T0333955

Achievement Relocked

Playful Thinking

Jesper Juul, Geoffrey Long, William Uricchio, and Mia Consalvo, editors

Achievement Relocked

Loss Aversion and Game Design

Geoffrey Engelstein

The MIT Press
Cambridge, Massachusetts
London, England

This book was set in Stone Serif and Stone Sans by Westchester Publishing Services. Printed and bound in the United States of America.

Library of Congress Cataloging-in-Publication Data

Names: Engelstein, Geoffrey, author.
Title: Achievement relocked : loss aversion and game design / Geoffrey Engelstein.
Description: Cambridge, MA : The MIT Press, [2019] | Series: Playful thinking | Includes bibliographical references and index.
Identifiers: LCCN 2019018577 | ISBN 9780262043533 (hardcover)
Subjects: LCSH: Video games--Design. | Computer games--Design. | Loss aversion. | Video games--Psychological aspects. | Computer games--Psychological aspects.
Classification: LCC GV1469.3 .E655 2019 | DDC 794.8/3--dc23
LC record available at https://lccn.loc.gov/2019018577

10 9 8 7 6 5 4 3 2 1

To Brian and Sydney,
for turning losses into gains.

Contents

On Thinking Playfully

Many people (we series editors included) find video games exhilarating, but it can be just as interesting to ponder why that is so. What do video games do? What can they be used for? How do they work? How do they relate to the rest of the world? Why is play both so important and so powerful?

Playful Thinking is a series of short, readable, and argumentative books that share some playfulness and excitement with the games that they are about. Each book in the series is small enough to fit in a backpack or coat pocket, and each combines depth with readability for any reader interested in playing more thoughtfully or thinking more playfully. This includes, but is by no means limited to, academics, game makers, and curious players.

We are casting our net wide. Each book in our series provides a blend of new insights and interesting arguments with overviews of knowledge from game studies and other areas. You will see this reflected not just in the range of titles in our series, but in the range of authors creating them. Our basic assumption is simple: video games are such a flourishing medium that any new perspective on them is likely to show us things unseen or forgotten, including those from such unconventional voices as artists, philosophers, or specialists in other industries or fields of study. These books are bridge builders, cross-pollinating areas with new knowledge and new ways of thinking.

At its heart, this is what Playful Thinking is all about: new ways of thinking about games and new ways of using games to think about the rest of the world.

Jesper Juul
Geoffrey Long
William Uricchio
Mia Consalvo

Preface

For over ten years, I have done a segment called GameTek for the *Dice Tower* podcast. In this short segment, I take an aspect of math, science, psychology, history, or another discipline and relate it to the world of gaming. In the process of researching GameTek topics, I've encountered a wide variety of psychology experiments that all point back to a core facet of the human experience: loss aversion. I'm pleased to bring all these disparate threads into a single volume, to give designers another lens with which to view their designs.

The ideas presented in this book would not have been possible without many discussions with colleagues, students, and friends. My *Ludology* cohosts Ryan Sturm, Mike Fitzgerald, and Gil Hova were invaluable for challenging my ideas and bringing up examples and counterexamples. Thanks also to my game design colleagues Andrew Parks, Tim Fowers, Isaac Shalev, Mark Herman, Rob Daviau, Eric Zimmerman, Frank Lantz, Sen-Foong Lim, Grant Rodiek, Cole Wehrle, Ignacy Trzewiczek, and so many others. Tom Vasel provided the platform of the *Dice Tower* podcast, which allowed these ideas to germinate, and Josh Gaylord provided invaluable editorial and content commentary during the writing of this book.

Thanks also to the students in my New York University classes over the years, who have been subjected to a wide variety of the games and surveys mentioned in this book.

Finally, thanks to my children and codesigners Brian and Sydney for being sounding boards and keeping me connected with modern video game culture, and to my wife Susan for pushing me to write this book.

Introduction

Games are artificial. At their root, they are activities in which players agree to place obstacles in the way of achieving a goal. By doing this, they mutually collaborate to create a "magic circle" within which modes of action and interaction are strictly proscribed. A game must be designed. It is not something that is discovered; it is constructed.

Storytelling is another human construction that shares many characteristics with game design. Although there are various motivations for telling stories, including teaching about other people and places, giving examples of behaviors to emulate, and providing morals, the primary goal of the storyteller is to create emotion in the listener—to create for them an *experience*.

Similarly, game designers ultimately try to create an experience for their players. A game experience can be similar to a story, in which the players see the plot from the inside and can make choices that impact the final outcome—such as *Star Wars: Knights of the Old Republic*,[1] in which they choose between the dark and light sides. Games can give players the ability to step into shoes they might not normally occupy, like a city manager in *SimCity*,[2] the head of a utility company in Power Grid,[3] or the leader of a noble house in *Crusader Kings*.[4]

But the designer does not need a traditional story framework or larger context to give players an experience. Games can tap into emotional needs as well, to put them into specific frames of mind. Chess makes players feel cerebral and in control; Magic: The Gathering[5] makes players feel clever; *Diablo*[6] makes players feel powerful; and *Mass Effect*[7] makes them feel heroic. They can also explore interpersonal emotions, as is done in the board game... *and then, we held hands.*[8] In this sense, games occupy a similar place to film and can draw on emotional impact as well as story elements to create the desired player experience.

One of the challenges of game design is that the tools available to the storyteller or composer do not always work in the context of a game. An author can strictly control the type and manner of information that is conveyed to the reader. Composers can leverage the direct link between music and emotions and, although subject to the interpretation of performers, dictate the content of the music. But games allow players to participate in the creation of the experience, to make choices, or to be subject to random forces outside of their control. Greg Costikyan, in *Uncertainty in Games*,[9] makes a compelling case that games are defined by uncertainty. If the moves and outcome of a game are known in advance, there is little point in playing. In contrast, the same story or song can be read or listened to over and over and still yield enjoyment.

The game designer creates a framework within which the players are free to operate. When compared with the author-reader relationship, game designers are a step removed from the players. The uncertainties present in the progress of the game prevent the designer from having full control over the experience of the players. How, therefore, does the designer give the targeted experience? How can the emotions of the players be nudged in the desired direction?

Theme, graphic design, and artwork can create ambiance and put players in the right frame of mind, but they may not be enough to sustain the desired emotional involvement. Another key technique is to leverage the very thing that separates the game designer from the players: choice. Player choice is a tool that is not available to the author or composer. Only in game design do we set before the players a series of options and rely on them to make choices that move the game forward—and into different and hopefully interesting directions.

A designer's understanding of the psychology of choice therefore is critical for manipulating the player's emotional state. This is a tool that can be used to guide players from a distance. It is through choices that players can be made tense, excited, frustrated, or sad.

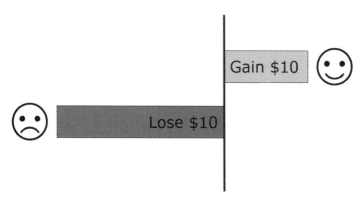

Figure 0.1
Loss aversion.

Loss aversion is a core concept in the psychology of choice. Here's the idea:

- Getting something makes you feel good.
- Losing something makes you feel bad.
- Losing something makes you feel worse than gaining the same thing makes you feel good.

For example, finding ten dollars feels good, and losing ten dollars feels bad—but on an "intensity of feeling" scale, losing is more intense (see figure 0.1). From this simple concept, a wide variety of psychological phenomena arise—leading to a wealth of techniques for the designer.

This book explores these phenomena, giving examples of how they are used and misused in game design. The point is not to say that technique X is good or that technique Y should be avoided. It is to explain how certain design elements will make players feel. It is up to the designer then to decide how best to apply those techniques.

1 Loss Aversion

This is a book about games, so let's start by playing one. You and I each take out ten dollars and put it on the table between us. Then we flip a coin, and the winner gets all the money. The loser gets nothing.

Would you play this game? If you're like most people, you would not. Or if you did agree to play, you wouldn't be super excited about it. You'd be worried about the prospect of losing your money.

Let's sweeten the offer a little and change things up. I'll put eleven dollars on the table against your ten dollars. If you lose, you still lose ten dollars. But if you win, you win eleven dollars.

Would you play now? Most folks still decline.

What about if you stand to gain twelve dollars against losing ten dollars? What about twenty dollars? Fifty dollars? One hundred dollars? At what point do you decide to play?

This illustrates the psychological concept of loss aversion. As discussed in the introduction, loss aversion can be expressed as follows:

Losing something makes you feel worse than gaining the same thing makes you feel good.

This is the essence of loss aversion. To be clear, the loss we are talking about is not losing the game itself, like being checkmated in chess or eliminated from the map in Risk. This is about losing elements within the game—sometimes tangible, sometimes intangible. Expressed another way:

The prospect of losing something weighs more heavily in our decision-making than the prospect of gaining something.

Loss aversion is at the root of a wide variety of human emotions, behaviors, and decision-making processes. It particularly manifests when a person needs to make a decision, like whether to play the coin flip game that opened this chapter. Games are a distinct form of art and entertainment in the way that they engage the players' attention and enable them to make decisions to change the outcome and shape their experience. And so loss aversion is a key part of the psychology of games.

Reading a book, watching a movie, or looking at a painting are all essentially passive activities. Although the reader of a book brings their own experiences and collaborates with the author to infuse the story with life, there are no active decisions being made.

Choice and decision-making are critical components of games. As such, it is very beneficial for game designers and players to understand the underlying psychology behind that decision-making, and loss aversion is a key characteristic of that. By thoroughly understanding the different manifestations of loss aversion, designers can subtly (and sometimes not so subtly) manipulate the player experience and create highly emotional decisions and game situations for the player—or design the game to give the players a calmly enjoyable time by avoiding loss aversion situations or framing them appropriately.

In 1979, psychologists Daniel Kahneman and Amos Tversky asked a series of questions as part of a study of people's approach to risk, which ultimately led to their discovery and formalization of loss aversion.[1] To gain a more in-depth understanding of the basic phenomenon, and to start putting some numbers on the impact, let's look at some experiments they performed.

Here's a typical choice they offered subjects:

Option A	An 80 percent chance of winning $4,000 and a 20 percent chance of winning nothing.
Option B	A 100 percent chance of winning $3,000.

What would you pick? If you chose option B, you're in good company. Of those surveyed, 80 percent chose B. Even when people are explicitly told that the expectation value[2] of option A is $3,200, $200 more than option B, they still select B.

Here's another set of options:

Option C	An 80 percent chance of *losing* $4,000 and a 20 percent chance of losing nothing.
Option D	A 100 percent chance of *losing* $3,000.

What choice do you make now? In surveys, a staggering 92 percent of people chose option C.

These and similar questions allow us to state a general principle:

People prefer a sure gain over a gamble for a larger gain, but they will gamble to avoid a sure loss.

This result goes against one of the fundamental axioms of economics: that people will act in a manner that benefits their best interests. In economics, the perfectly rational actor is known as *Homo economicus*. It was first proposed in the nineteenth century and was the basis of many early economic theories, and it was assumed that it was a good representation of how people act. But in the latter half of the twentieth century, the accuracy of *Homo economicus* began to crumble, and these experimental results were part of that. Tversky and Kahneman's paper "Prospect Theory: An Analysis of Decision under Risk" is considered one of the seminal works of behavioral economics, and ultimately Kahneman was awarded the Nobel Prize for this work.

In both the A/B and C/D pairs given previously, people consistently and overwhelmingly select the path that will lead to *smaller* average gains and *larger* average losses. As noted, when the probabilities of things happening are high (80 percent and 100 percent in these examples), people will choose a sure gain over a chance of a larger gain but will gamble to avoid a sure loss.

As the chances of something happening become very small, though, people's attitudes change. Here are two more sets of choices to illustrate this situation:

Option A	A 0.2 percent chance to win $3,000.
Option B	A 0.1 percent chance to win $6,000.

and

Option C	A 0.2 percent chance to lose $3,000.
Option D	A 0.1 percent chance to lose $6,000.

Here, all the options have the same expectation value. But people gravitate toward the riskier gains and the less risky losses. Seventy-three percent of people choose B, which gives a smaller chance to win a bigger amount, and 70 percent choose C, which has a larger chance to lose a smaller amount. Things are exactly flipped from the earlier questions. When chances are low, people will gamble for a bigger win and will accept a slightly higher risk to avoid a big loss.

When people see very low probabilities, they mentally lump them together. The brain sees 0.1 percent and 0.2 percent as basically the same thing—even though one is twice as large as the other. You do not see this as the same as picking between a 10 percent choice and a 20 percent choice, and certainly not the same as 40 percent and 80 percent.

This is a key principal of the lottery. The probabilities are so incredibly small that people just don't have a concept of what it means. Lotteries have been pushing the chances of winning the big jackpot progressively lower and lower because people focus on the top-line prize of the jackpot and have no idea of the odds or what the odds really mean. In July 2015, Powerball (a US-based lottery) changed the rules so that the odds of getting the top prize were reduced from 1 in 175 million to 1 in 292 million[3]—which makes it less likely someone will win each week, driving the jackpot higher. High jackpots can lead to huge spikes in ticket sales and profits.

Lotteries take advantage of this innate overestimation of low-probability events. Playing the Powerball jackpot gives you the following odds:

| Option A | A 99.999999997 percent chance of losing $1. |
| Option B | A 0.000000003 percent chance of winning $1 million. |

People don't really understand B—certainly not the probability. They focus on the dollar figure, and that's what makes it an acceptable wager; that's what allows people to overcome their loss aversion.

On the high end of the probability scale, humans give very special significance to 100 percent. The lure of the "sure thing" is very compelling. Think back to the first choice set in this section:

Option A	An 80 percent chance of winning $4,000 and a 20 percent chance of winning nothing.
Option B	A 100 percent chance of winning $3,000.

The 100 percent chance of winning $3,000 is very hard to resist. Even if you change it as follows:

Option A	A 99 percent chance of winning $4,000 and a 1 percent chance of winning nothing.
Option B	A 100 percent chance of winning $3,000.

Many will still gravitate to B. Loss aversion creates potential negative psychological effects that people will go to great lengths to avoid. Better to just have peace of mind and pocket the $3,000 rather than regret that you hit that 1 percent chance and ended up with nothing.

So we can state these key principles:

- People prefer sure gains over a chance for a larger gain.
- People will take a risk to avoid a sure loss.
- People treat all small probabilities the same and just compare the gain or loss.
- Both 100 percent and 0 percent are special.

Losing Levels

A lesson that video game designers have learned over the years is to reward players. Creating a tight action–reward loop gives the player a sense of progress, creates habit-forming activities, and keeps the player engaged and coming back for more. These rewards can take a variety of forms, including gaining levels and earning special achievements for certain activities.

Achievements have been around in different forms since the early days of video gaming. Arguably the "intermissions" in *Pac-Man*[4] and *Ms. Pac-Man*[5] serve a similar function: giving the player a reward for achieving a certain stage, albeit one that needs to be obtained again the next time the game is played.

The codification of achievements came with the advent of the Xbox 360 and Steam, which made it easy for developers to create achievements and allowed players to compare them with the achievements of their friends. The phrase *achievement unlocked* entered popular vernacular as a synonym for reaching a goal.

Throughout the modern era of the achievement, there has been one constant: Achievements, once obtained, cannot be taken away. Achievements are never "relocked." This is an expectation of all video gamers, and the author is not aware of any violations of this principle. It isn't hard to imagine the emotional impact it would have on players if this principle was violated. There have been achievements that are shown to the player but are impossible to achieve[6]—but not any that are taken away. Perhaps a future designer will leverage this in a creative and dynamic way.

One of the earliest computer role-playing games (RPGs) was *Wizardry,*[7] for the Apple II computer. Along with the *Ultima* series,[8] *Wizardry* established many of the concepts that carry over to today's games. It was the first computer RPG with a first-person perspective, the first that allowed the player to control a party of characters, and the first to establish a turn-based system of combat that survives to this day in games like *Darkest Dungeon*.[9]

There was, however, one feature of *Wizardry* that did not survive.

Like pretty much every RPG, *Wizardry* borrowed liberally from Dungeons & Dragons (D&D).[10] One of those borrowed concepts was that of experience points (XP) and character levels. As monsters were defeated, characters earned XP—and when enough XP were accumulated, characters advanced to the next level, gaining better abilities, spells, and health.

Many monsters in *Wizardry* had special abilities: breath weapons that attacked multiple characters at once, poison that made characters lose health with each step they took, even a ninja with an *insta-kill* attack, meaning one hit could kill a character. But even more feared were the few monsters that had *level drain*. If these creatures hit one of your characters, in addition to normal damage there was a chance that you would lose a level of experience and all the bonuses you had gained. If you were unlucky enough, a single character could go down multiple levels in a single battle.

Why was this more feared than insta-kill? Death was curable in *Wizardry*. There was a spell you could cast to resurrect dead characters. But there was no easy or quick recovery from losing a level. You just had to earn the lost experience points back. And because it was 1982, the game stored the characters on a 5.25″ floppy disk. Due to the copy protection that was being used, there was no easy way to back up characters. If something happened to your characters, it was, for all practical purposes, permanent.

This type of loss did not sit well with players. In one sense, it was frustrating simply because of the lost time. You could get back to where you were before; you just needed to invest the time. And often that time was not much more significant than what was required to defeat particularly challenging monsters, for which the player had to repeatedly retreat from the battle, regroup, and reengage.

Of more concern was the loss of spells and abilities. You had gained new toys, and now the game was taking them away from you. Loss aversion makes this a huge negative for player psychology.

The TVTropes website has an entry for Level Drain[11] in general as a mechanic, and it specifically calls out *Wizardry*: "The *Wizardry* games had monsters that caused [level draining] on your party, which was part of what made the series so infamously difficult, as the player then had to get the characters out of the area they were now too low levelled to survive in, and then grind back up before they could return, and then pray that their levels weren't lost again."

I last played *Wizardry* in 1984, and I can personally attest to the reader that the psychological blow of losing character levels still sends a shiver down my spine (see figure 1.1).

Level draining as a game mechanic goes back to the foundational RPG Dungeons & Dragons. In D&D, many undead creatures, like wraiths and wights, had level drain as an ability. The history of Dungeons & Dragons shows a gradual lessening of the severity of level drain. In Advanced Dungeons & Dragons (AD&D), the first mass-market version of the game, level drain was included as an undead ability and could not be saved against. In other words, if a character suffered level drain, they lost a level, and that was it.

In later versions, D&D third edition and version "3.5," level drain was modified by allowing players to make a saving roll to prevent a level loss. But if the roll failed, the level was permanently lost.

Figure 1.1
A character losing a level in *Wizardry*.

In fourth and subsequent editions, level drain was completely removed. The undead creatures that used to have it now put effects on characters like *weaken* and *immobilize*—which could be cured through normal means within the game.

The release of fourth edition Dungeons & Dragons was controversial because it made radical changes to the underlying system (separate from the removal of level drain). In response, Paizo Inc. launched the Pathfinder roleplaying game, which was intended to be a direct descendant of D&D 3.5, including almost all the mechanics of that game. Yet even Pathfinder completely eliminated level drain as a mechanic.

To give you some idea of player discussions about level drain, here are excerpts from a blog post and comments from 2012:

> I was discussing level draining the other day with my D&D group. My players are adamantly opposed to the concept of level draining

undead. I never used to be. In fact, I was thinking "come on, pansies! This is part of the game. Deal with it!" After all, it can't be THAT bad. It's a hallmark of old school gaming. Watch out for that Wight!

Another post responded:

I used to feel this way, but I've since come around (somewhat) to the idea of level draining. This mostly came from reading somewhere that level-draining monsters are not creatures to be fought, they are obstacles to be avoided (if used correctly). *There is little you can do in D&D to viscerally terrify players, but for whatever reason level draining does it.* And undead are supposed to be terrifying. (emphasis mine)

Another post highlights the emotional aspect:

Many players…would rather die than lose 50% of their XP. Maybe that is a more emotional than sensible reaction, but many players feel that way.

As does this:

What I've always liked about the level drain is just how personal that loss can be; as if part of the character's life truly was just ripped away forever, lessening them for it.

The loss aversion aspect of level drain is clear in these comments. This is an emotional response from the players, and it does not come purely from a rational place. There is something deeper here than simply the lost time. As the final excerpt noted, it's "as if part of the character's life was just ripped away." The anguish from losing a level far outweighs the excitement of gaining one.

If players were offered the opportunity to fight a creature with a fifty-fifty chance of either gaining an entire level or losing an entire level, I'm quite confident that almost all would pass it up.

Game designers have learned this lesson, and this type of loss is, for the most part, scrupulously avoided. The standard now is that once an ability is gained, it is never lost. It may be superseded, improved, or upgraded, or negative effects may be applied, but it is not taken away from the player. In Blizzard's RPG *Dia-blo*, as an example, there is no way to lose a level or ability once gained. Items can be lost or damaged, but not levels or abilities.

Tracking

For our next example of loss aversion in gaming, let's look at a card from *Hearthstone*, a game from Blizzard Entertainment, released in 2014 (see figure 1.2). This is a two-player online collectible card game, similar to the physical card game Magic: The Gathering. Before the game starts, players construct a deck of thirty cards from their collections and then do battle against each other.

To win, players must reduce their opponent's health to zero by playing creatures and spells. Each turn, a player draws one card from their deck. If they need to draw a card, but all their cards are gone, instead they suffer fatigue damage. This damage starts at one the first time you need to draw, and it increases each time you need to draw but cannot. This mechanism prevents games from continuing forever—and presents players with a strategic option to create a deck that adds cards to their own deck during play or forces opponents to draw or discard additional cards so they will start taking fatigue damage sooner. However, the majority of games do not end with a player exhausting their deck; one player typically wins before either deck runs out.

The Tracking card has the following effect:

> **Look at the top three cards of your deck. Draw one and discard the others.**

When you play Tracking, it shows you three cards and you select one to keep. The other two are gone from the game forever.

Although every player gets this card as part of the starter set, it's rarely used by beginning *Hearthstone* players, and it's

Figure 1.2
Tracking card from *Hearthstone*.

controversial in the forums. Here is a comment from the website
Hearthpwn, a popular *Hearthstone* fan site:

> I see the use of Tracking, but psychologically I've always disliked the
> idea of burning two cards to get a third. If I put a card in my deck
> it means I wanted to use it, not to discard it in favour of something
> else.

And another:

> Tracking: Burn 2 other cards to draw 1 and possibly lose key parts of
> your deck!

Tracking, however, is a very good card, and a staple of high-level play. Players who are not fans of Tracking focus on the two cards that are being discarded, primarily raising two concerns:

1. You will exhaust your deck before your opponent and suffer more fatigue damage.
2. If you draw three very good cards, you will have to lose two of them from the game.

The first point is easily refuted for those familiar with the game because very few games go to fatigue, and this card is only usable in hunter decks. Hunter decks are very damage-focused, so games tend to be won or lost quickly. So discarding the two extra cards really has little impact on the game, as it will typically end with more than ten cards remaining in the deck.

The second objection—that you don't have access to the cards you are forced to discard—is the real issue, as illustrated in the quotes highlighted earlier. At its heart are loss aversion and, more specifically, regret, which we'll cover in detail in chapter 6. Players do not like being forced to discard cards. Some people suggest that if you use Tracking, you should include multiples of all your best cards to lessen the chances that you will have to discard all of them.

And yet, from a mathematical and gameplay perspective, this concern is demonstrably baseless. Unless the game goes to fatigue, at its conclusion you will have, typically, ten or more cards remaining in your deck. You very rarely see all your cards in a game of *Hearthstone* anyway. With Tracking, you basically get advance notice of two of those leftover cards—which gives you an opportunity to improve your strategy because you have a slightly better chance of knowing what you will draw.

As a thought experiment, let's try to frame this effect another way. Let's change the card to say this:

> **Look at the top three cards. Keep one and shuffle the other two back into your deck. Then discard the bottom two cards in your deck without looking at them.**

I showed this option along with the original to a variety of *Hearthstone* players, and in general they were much happier with this effect. The cards are discarded unseen, and they are coming from the bottom of the deck. Now it's much clearer to players that it was unlikely that they would play these cards in any case. Also, because the cards are discarded without being seen, regret is to a large extent avoided. There is no way to view the discard pile in *Hearthstone*, so unless you go through your entire deck you will never have any idea which cards were discarded.

Most players psychologically prefer this version of Tracking. However, from a gameplay standpoint it's definitely worse. Knowing which cards have been discarded helps your play. If you know that a certain card is gone from the game, you can tailor your strategy accordingly rather than basing your play on the hope that you draw it. Discarding unseen hurts the player, and yet it's preferred by most.

Tracking creates anxiety in players, particularly beginners. Designers have the opportunity to present this card in a way that is more palatable but less powerful. Depending on the desired emotional effect, it may make sense either to leave it as it is or to use a tweaked version.

Triggering loss aversion, with its attendant anxiety, is not a priori something to be avoided. The goal of this book is not to say that things should be done one way or another. It is simply to create awareness of what impact certain choices can have. It is to give a tool to designers that they can use to manipulate the emotional state of the player and subtly guide player choices.

Casino Games

Casinos are in the business of getting people to risk losses for possible gains. As such, they need to overcome our inherent psychological loss aversion. Casinos use a variety of techniques that are useful for the game designer to understand.

One of the first things you do when entering a casino is exchange your money for chips. This creates an abstraction layer between the physical object (the chip) and the value it represents. Money becomes "points," which alleviates some of the anxiety that people apply to losing money. Studies show that abstract representations of value, like chips and tokens, do not trigger the same fear of loss.[12]

It also immediately creates a separation from your money. It is almost as if the player has taken a partial step toward losing the money. It's already something separate from the rest of the money in your wallet or bank account. This is emphasized by the fact that you need to go through additional steps to turn it back into real money.

Cleverly, you can exchange money into chips basically anywhere in a casino. If I sit down at a blackjack table, I can give $200 to the dealer and get chips. But if I want to get my $200 back, I need to go to a separate area in the casino, typically on the margins, and wait in line to turn it back in. This extra step creates a psychological barrier to turning the chips back into cash and so gives the casino another chance to entice players to stay at their current table or slot machine or to be attracted to another game during the walk to the redemption area—or to entice them to simply not cash in the chips at all and save them for a future visit. Chips are also only good in a single location: the casino where they are obtained. They are imprinted with the name of the casino and cannot be used elsewhere. The extra step to turn them back into money must be taken before you leave to recover their value. If players simply played with cash, it would be much easier to come and go at a casino and to leave when they were ready.

The idea of chips has been adopted by a variety of online games in which you turn actual real-world currency into in-game currency. For example, in *League of Legends*,[13] you can purchase *Riot points* that allow you to obtain skins, unlock new characters, and get other in-game materials. Once you purchase points, they are simply shown in your account as points. The dollar figure is wiped away, so the cost of items is somewhat obscured. However, these systems are not completely analogous because this is a one-way trip. There is no way to convert riot points (or other currencies in games that utilize the same system, like the ISK currency of *Eve Online*[14]) back to real-world currency.

The Blizzard game *Heroes of the Storm*[15] originally allowed players to purchase items with real money, but in 2017 the system changed to force players to purchase an intermediate currency to obtain items. Further muddying the waters, there are three currencies in the game—gold, gems, and shards—and they are earned and spent in different ways.

Jackpots (high-odds bets) are another method used to overcome loss aversion. As discussed earlier, people approach low-probability/high-reward events differently than more probable events. Going back to an earlier example:

| Option A | A 0.2 percent chance to win $3,000. |
| Option B | A 0.1 percent chance to win $6,000. |

When people are presented with this choice, three out of four select option B.

People are not good at judging low-probability events. Once probabilities get low, people tend to put them into the same mental bucket—and the loss aversion equation flips. People will more readily make a low-probability/high-payoff bet.

Casinos are acutely aware of the allure of jackpots. The core of classic casino games—craps, roulette, and blackjack—are structured around fifty-fifty games, with small rules modifications to give the house an edge.[16] There have always been side bets, particularly in craps and roulette, but these have proliferated in recent years. There are now many jackpot-style bets in almost all games as casinos cater to the desire for these long shots.

In addition to high-odds side bets, there is also a proliferation of new games that typically have more complex rules than the classics. For example, different varieties of poker are increasingly popular. These often have charts of odds that are paid out for different poker hands—with a huge payout for a royal flush—and games of multiple stages with decisions at each stage.

The complexity of these games makes it difficult, if not impossible, for most people to be able to judge what the actual odds are. Roulette is relatively easy to understand in terms of what payouts should be for different bets, and, even for the less math savvy, there are many resources that explain roulette and how it works. These new casino games, on the other hand, force players to make the judgments themselves, and we typically judge incorrectly.

The Rest of the Book

There are many aspects of human psychology that relate to loss aversion. In the rest of the book, we explore several of these and the way they allow us to look at different aspects of game design. Many of these ideas are interrelated. Let's take a brief look at the upcoming chapters and the concepts under consideration. Having a basic understanding in place will give context for each concept.

Chapter 2: Endowment Effect

When an object is yours, it gains value, psychologically, over an equivalent object that is not yours. Owning something makes it more valuable to you, simply by virtue of it being "yours." This is referred to as the *endowment effect*.

We explore this effect with a close examination of the Weighted Companion Cube from the game *Portal*. This case is particularly instructive. The designers found in testing that the players were not following the path they wanted them to, so the designers gradually introduced psychological cues until they got the players to carry a box from point A to point B. In doing so, they launched one of the most improbably beloved objects in video game history.

Chapter 3: Framing

As discussed earlier, people prefer a sure gain over gambling for a larger gain and prefer to gamble to avoid a sure loss. But in many situations, whether something is viewed as a gain or a loss can be manipulated. This is called *framing*. It is used in many gaming contexts to give the players specific emotional experiences and to subtly guide choices.

This chapter explores framing in the context of tabletop games and their evolution through the twentieth century, as well as the way that top eSports games like *League of Legends* and *Counterstrike* use framing in positive and negative ways.

Chapter 4: Utility Theory

In our first monetary example earlier in this chapter, there was a choice between a guaranteed gain of $3,000 or an 80 percent chance of getting $4,000. Mathematically, the 80 percent chance of gaining $4,000 is better, but most people choose the guarantee of $3,000.

One way of looking at this, other than loss aversion, is by exploring the impact the gain will have on someone's life. Winning $3,000 or $4,000 feels the same in terms of how it will impact your life. As the numbers get bigger, they can get further apart, and most people will still lump them together. For example, winning $50,000,000 or $100,000,000 are basically equivalent for almost all people. Either amount will change your life.

The study of this is called *utility theory*. It focuses not just on maximizing what you're getting but on how things impact you. Utility theory has been exploited in a variety of games. Perhaps the most notable and accessible is the game show *Deal or No Deal*. In this chapter, we dive deeper into the specific ways that *Deal or No Deal* uses utility theory to create a tense and entertaining game.

Although the first four chapters focus on the loss or gain of money or objects, albeit virtual objects, for the final chapters of the book we turn our attention to activities, decisions, and achievements. These are also subject to loss aversion, but they express themselves in different ways. Because games are so heavily based on player choices and decisions, an understanding of player psychology is instructive for both designers and players.

Chapter 5: Endowed Progress

A 2006 study looked at ways of motivating people to complete a task. At a car wash, the researchers handed out two different loyalty cards. The first one had eight spots for stamps. Each time you got a car wash, you earned a stamp. Getting all eight stamps awarded you a free car wash.

The second card had ten spots for stamps, but the first two were already stamped, so it also required eight more car washes to get the free car wash. The amount of investment required by customers was exactly the same.

But the results were not. The cards with eight stamps were redeemed 19 percent of the time. Those with two free "starter" stamps were redeemed 34 percent of the time—almost twice as often.

This is called the *endowed progress* effect. The idea is that people are more likely to complete a task that has already been started rather than beginning a task from scratch. It is related to both loss aversion and the endowment effect, as people feel like they already have "ownership" of the task in some way—and so not completing it comes with a psychological cost.

We examine several games that use endowed progress to hook the players and motivate them to complete, or simply remain involved in, the game and the community around the game.

Chapter 6: Regret and Competence

Regret is defined as the negative feeling resulting from a choice that has gone badly. It is a powerful emotion, and it is the driver behind many loss aversion effects. In many ways, loss aversion can be explained as a way to minimize regret.

Several clever experiments have been performed to quantify regret, allowing us to explore different ways in which people make decisions and how these impact people's regret. This chapter explores those experiments and looks at the way regret is

harnessed within games to drive emotional impact or to manipulate the mechanics so that players do not feel as much regret
when things do not go their way.

Competence is another emotional element of decision-
making, related to how much we understand about the choices
we are making. In behavioral psychology, *Competence* has a specific meaning. It is not about how good someone is at an activity. It is about the knowledge that a player has about the world
of the activity. It is the ratio of what you know versus what can
possibly be known.

The way a game is structured can have a big impact on the
competence that players feel. Depending on the emotional effect
desired, subtle changes can make a big difference. In this chapter, we look at some specific examples of these design decisions
in both tabletop and video games.

Chapter 7: Putting It All Together

In the final chapter, we pull together the various threads with an
in-depth look at a series of popular games and how they evolved.

2   Endowment Effect

In an experiment, conducted by Knetsch and Sinden,[1] participants were given either two dollars or a lottery ticket (with a
retail cost of two dollars). Later, they were offered an opportunity to trade the two dollars for a lottery ticket or vice versa. Very
few chose to make the trade. People were happy with the status
quo, whether they had the cash or the ticket. Other experiments
showed that when people have something in their possession, it
gains value in their mind. In economic and psychological circles,
this tendency to give something more value because it belongs
to you is called the *endowment effect*, a term coined by Thaler.[2]

The endowment effect is an issue for classical economic
theory, because the *Homo economicus* theory assumes purely
rational actions by people when valuing things. If something
gains more value just because you have it, that throws a lot of
theories out of whack. Therefore, researchers have been trying
to measure this effect in more detail and figure out its origins.

The lottery ticket experiment has been duplicated many
times with a variety of products and exchange conditions. For
example, in one experiment students were given mugs and then
later given the option to exchange them for chocolate bars. The
rate at which students make this trade is well below what would

be expected based on a separate survey of whether they would rather receive a chocolate bar or mug. Intriguingly, the effect is not seen equally for all types of goods. In a similar experiment, participants were given a token, and told that at the end of the experiment they would be given a mug for their token. They were then offered a chocolate bar for their token, and the endowment effect did not happen.[3]

This is an interesting juxtaposition to our earlier discussion of casinos and their use of chips. These experiments emphasize the point that introducing an abstraction, like a token or a chip, blunts the effect of loss aversion and makes it easier for people to give up their possessions.

The endowment effect is seen not just in humans but also in chimpanzees[4]—but only with food, not with toys and other objects. This suggests that it may be a holdover from our evolutionary past and was originally focused on things key for survival.

This was further explored in 2008 by members of a team from Stanford University who did an endowment effect experiment while taking fMRI brain scans.[5] The location of brain activity during the decision-making process suggests that the endowment effect is tied to an emotional response to a sense of loss. The original explanation for the endowment effect was an offshoot of loss aversion, championed by Kahneman and Tversky. The theory was that the loss of the object hurts more than the cost of acquisition or than not getting it at all. Although the Stanford fMRI study supports this interpretation, there are other theoretical explanations that do not invoke loss aversion as a requirement. Regardless of the source, the effect itself has been demonstrated experimentally many times and is worth discussing here.

Weighted Companion Cube

The game *Portal*[6] offers an informative illustration of the concept of the endowment effect.

Portal is a puzzle game in which the player needs to complete a series of levels called *test chambers*. The game is centered around a special weapon called the *portal gun*, which allows the player to place two connecting "portals" on walls, floors, and ceilings—one blue and one orange. The player can move between these portals and needs to use them to overcome obstacles and reach the exit of each test chamber.

Throughout the game, the players are both guided and taunted by GLaDOS, a malevolent AI that runs the test chambers. It becomes increasingly clear as the game progresses that GLaDOS, although initially helpful, is not actually trustworthy and may be insane.

In test chamber 2, the players are introduced to weighted storage cubes (see figure 2.1). These are similar to the ubiquitous crates present in so many games, including Valve's famous *Half-Life*. Unlike crates, though, these storage cubes cannot be smashed by the player. They are typically used as puzzle elements so that, for example, the player can place them on a button that activates and holds open a door while the player moves through it.

Various test chambers that use weighted storage cubes as puzzle elements also incorporate force fields that the player can move through, but cubes cannot. If the player is carrying a cube and passes through a force field, the cube is destroyed and resets back to its starting position. This technique allows the level designers to force the players to come up with creative solutions to solve certain areas without using a cube or to figure out a way

Figure 2.1
Portal's weighted storage cube.

to get the cube into the area they need it in without passing through a force field.

In test chamber 17, GLaDOS introduces the player to a new type of cube: the Weighted Companion Cube (see figure 2.2). It is, in all ways, exactly the same as the standard weighted storage cubes the player has become accustomed to—except that it has a heart on the sides instead of the Aperture Science symbol (the logo of the fictional company that runs the test facility).

The Weighted Companion Cube is introduced by GLaDOS with these words: "The vital apparatus stand will deliver a Weighted Companion Cube in 3, 2, 1.... This Weighted Companion Cube will accompany you through the test chamber. Please take care of it." The player then must maneuver the cube through the test chamber to complete the test successfully.

Figure 2.2
Weighted Companion Cube.

During the level, GLaDOS says: "The symptoms most commonly produced by Enrichment Center testing are superstition, perceiving inanimate objects as alive, and hallucinations. The Enrichment Center reminds you that the Weighted Companion Cube will never threaten to stab you and, in fact, cannot speak. In the event that the Weighted Companion Cube does speak, the Enrichment Center urges you to disregard its advice." Near the end of the level, the player reaches a room with an incinerator, and GLaDOS announces: "You did it! The Weighted Companion Cube certainly brought you good luck. However, it cannot accompany you for the rest of the test and, unfortunately, must be euthanized. Please escort your Weighted Companion Cube to the Aperture Science Emergency Intelligence Incinerator."

Figure 2.3
Emergency intelligence incinerator.

To proceed and complete the level, the player must drop the Companion Cube into the incinerator (see figure 2.3). If you hesitate, GLaDOS prods you: "Rest assured that an independent panel of ethicists has absolved the Enrichment Center, Aperture Science employees, and all test subjects of any moral responsibility for the Companion Cube euthanizing process." Finally, when you do drop the cube into the incinerator, it drops out of sight and you are told: "You euthanized your faithful Companion Cube more quickly than any test subject on record. Congratulations!"

Given its minor role in the game—just one level out of nineteen (and not a particularly long one)—the Weighted Companion Cube was the breakout star of *Portal*. It inspired plush toys, t-shirts, cosplay, and a much larger role in *Portal 2*,[7] and it was a key character in the comic series *Portal 2: Lab Rat*.

The game designers themselves were a little surprised at the intensity of the reaction. In an interview conducted by *Games for Windows* magazine[8] shortly after the game released, they expressed a certain level of amazement:

GFW: You were that confident the Companion Cube gag would go over well?

Kim Swift, Level Designer: We knew they'd like it, but not how much they'd like it.

Jeep Barnett, Programmer: Dude, we didn't know they'd become obsessive.

KS: Someone at rockpapershotgun.com painted his freezer to look like a Companion Cube.

In the same interview, they offered more reaction and theorized about why the Companion Cube might be popular:

GFW: Why is this particular aspect resonating with people?

JB: You're alone through the entire game, and the Cube is your one and only companion. I'm not sure.

GFW: Was the incineration idea inspired in part by the infamous Milgram experiment?

KS: Not particularly. We had a long level called Box Marathon; we wanted players to bring this box with them from the beginning to the end. But people would forget about the box, so we added dialogue, applied the heart to the cube, and continued to up the ante until people became attached to the box. Later on, we added the incineration idea. The artistic expression grew from the gameplay.

Swift later relates that "A couple of people jumped into the incinerator themselves rather than kill the Cube."

The *Portal* team proposes two reasons here:

The first is *isolation*. There are few characters in *Portal*. Other than the player character, who does not speak and is only glimpsed through portals, there is the disembodied voice of the AI, GLaDOS, who is clearly not on the player's side, and gun turrets that speak a series of canned lines and, of course, shoot at the player. Although endearing, they aren't particularly friendly.

The player, in a real way, is alone and isolated in the sterile test chamber environment of the game. This seems normal to the player, as it seems natural in the context of the game. However, as the game goes on, the fourth wall is broken, showing accidental glimpses of a gritty, behind-the-scenes world that contains graffiti from the test subjects who came before the player, including a series of images depicting the Companion Cube itself, portrayed as a friend. The revelation that there is a real world beyond the test chambers ultimately propels the player outside the boundaries of the game and into freedom.

So, several propose, the isolation of the player makes them long for companionship of any type—even that of an inanimate object. As Barnett speculates: "You're alone through the entire game, and the Cube is your one and only companion."

However, the brevity of your interaction with the Companion Cube—and the large number of other cubes—makes this an unsatisfying explanation. There are other characters in the game that do actually talk to you (GLaDOS and the sentry turrets). Although they are malevolent, they do speak with you and are charming.

The second explanation offered for the player's attachment to the Weighted Companion Cube is *personification*. If the Companion Cube were instead a standard cube, it would not have had the psychological impact it does. The player sees many, many standard cubes in the *Portal* world and uses them as tools to solve puzzles. They are destroyed at various points in the game and impart no emotional effect.

Interestingly, this issue led directly to the birth of the Companion Cube. In her comments, Swift alludes to this: "People would forget about the box, so we added dialogue, applied the heart to the cube, and continued to up the ante until people became attached to the box." The very lack of player attachment to standard cubes created a gameplay issue, which the designers cleverly resolved by personifying the cube.

Portal tries to turn the Companion Cube into a pet or a baby. This is a helpless creature that can't do anything on its own, that relies on you for protection and guidance. One of the few things GLaDOS says about the cube is "Please take care of it." This is evocative of the Rifleman's Creed, which is part of the US Marine Corps doctrine: "This is my rifle. There are many like it, but this one is mine. My rifle is my best friend. It is my life. I must master it as I must master my life." This creed tries to establish a relationship between the person and the weapon. In the world of *Portal*, cubes are anonymous and ubiquitous. At first glance, the same holds for rifles in the army. Yet it is important that the soldier treat the rifle with care and respect and not treat it as replaceable. This is the same challenge faced by the *Portal* designers, with far less serious consequences for failure, of course. It is instructive to see that they have hit upon similar solutions to forming an anthropomorphic relationship with an inanimate object.

In fact, the Rifleman's Creed goes even further than *Portal*. Whereas GLaDOS insists that the Companion Cube is not alive, the Rifleman's Creed says: "My rifle is human, even as I, because it is my life."

As a counterpoint, Terry Wolfe[9] proposes that the manipulative nature of the way the game presents the Weighted Companion Cube underlines the power of the moment. "In a sense, you, the player, really are the test subject." He says that the player is always aware of the manipulation and aware that they are playing a game, so the player is only "ironically" attached to the cube. It is at the moment of having to throw the cube into the incinerator that the player is forced either to step away from their attachment or choose emotional investment. In essence, the game *pushes* the player into an emotional reaction.

Ultimately, all these explanations feed into a single root cause: loss aversion and the endowment effect that it spawns. The player's first interaction with the Companion Cube is when they are literally endowed with it. It is presented as a gift that belongs specifically to them, and they are told that they need to take care of it. And through much of the level, the Companion Cube can start to feel like a burden. The player must constantly lift it and carry it and figure out how to get it past various obstacles. It does not feel like a friend.

The catalyzing moment in your relationship with the Companion Cube is when you have to throw it into the incinerator. The fact that *you* have to take that action is the emotional crux, and it's what triggers loss aversion in the player. If the cube simply disappeared at the end of the level, or if a claw came down and picked it up—even if you then saw it being incinerated—it would not have the same emotional impact.

This is why the isolation explanation falls short. The player does not truly form the attachment at the beginning or middle of the level. It is this completely unexpected act of cubicide that creates the emotional crisis and makes this such a memorable moment.

In future chapters, we will revisit this theme of the player making the choice to lose something rather than it being dictated by the computer or the game play. Without choice, the player may feel anger, but the longer-lasting emotions of loss and regret will not be invoked.

Robinson Crusoe and First Martians

The board game Robinson Crusoe[10] and its spiritual successor First Martians[11] both incorporate loss, but because of the thematic representation and the particulars of the endowment effect, they impacted players quite differently. Crusoe was released to great acclaim, moving into the top fifty games on the BoardGameGeek website (boardgamegeek.com) with an average rating of 7.9. It is a cooperative game in which the players are stranded on an island with next to no supplies and need to accomplish the scenario goal—for example, creating a signal fire, finding and rescuing someone, or avoiding a volcanic eruption. The game has a reputation for being extremely brutal and unforgiving. Here is an excerpt from a review titled "Yep, You're Doomed":

> Because there is so much to manage in Crusoe, any miscalculation is fatal in short order. Food and shelter are always issues, and it seems impossible to keep both in good supply. Any lack in either, and you're taking damage. One player dies, and you lose. Fail your scenario objective, you lose. Face it, you're going to lose.
>
> Worse, the only way to even hope to win is to take risks, and that means rolling the dice. You think dice hate you? Oh, baby, you haven't begun …
>
> Rolling dice racks up Event cards and damage. Event cards are almost always bad. Soon your Event card deck is filled with snakes ready to poison you, pumas following you back to camp, and on and on. Disease, pestilence, alligators, and …
>
> If you can't get the terrain you need, you can't invent items you need, and you die. If you try to split up your player's actions, you roll dice, and you die.

> If you use both your player actions to ensure success, you don't
> generate enough resources you need in the long run, and you die.
> Die, die, die.[12]

So the reviewer must have hated it, right? Well, after going
through a series of descriptions of all the unfortunate things that
happened to the players, he concludes with this statement:

> Crusoe is an achievement. Seriously, designer Trzewiczek should be
> congratulated on what may become a classic. Theme, play, feel, emo-
> tions generated—this game hits all the high points. It's the pinnacle
> of contemporary co-op games.

Several years later, publisher Portal (no relation to the *Portal*
game discussed earlier) released First Martians, a spiritual successor to Crusoe. In Martians, the players represent the first expedition to the red planet and need to complete the scenario goals,
which may be exploring an area, retrieving probes, or setting
up a base camp. The general mechanisms are similar to those in
Crusoe, albeit with different resources to manage, like oxygen.

The game was highly anticipated but upon release was not
well received, receiving an average rating of 6.8—a significant
drop from Crusoe. So why did Crusoe succeed in punishing the
players where Martians failed?

One of the main complaints about Martians centered on
loss—specifically, that things keep breaking down. In Martians,
you begin the game with a perfectly operational base (called the
HUB) in the game. Each turn, players roll dice and draw cards to
see which systems malfunction. Then one of the actions players
can take is to attempt to repair the malfunctions.

Although things also break in Crusoe, there is a clear difference in Martians. In Crusoe, players start with nothing and perform actions to create shelter, build tools, or construct a fire. In

Martians, you start with everything and things go downhill from there. The level of emotional investment in the things that you lose is much higher in Crusoe than Martians.

This emotional gap is not just because you are given everything in Martians rather than having to earn it. There also is no personality or identity to the HUB that connects players emotionally to it. Recall that to get players to become attached to the Companion Cube, the *Portal* designers added a heart to its artwork and included dialogue that defined the relationship. There is no such attempt in Martians. The HUB is just a control panel. It would have been possible to add an AI personality to the game and have the players read paragraphs that gave it dialogue and a connection to the players. There is even an associated app that could have been used for that purpose, but it was not done. Instead it was comparable to just a standard portal cube, which players do not become attached to.

Building your shelter in Crusoe, in contrast, greatly attaches the players do it. You need to gather materials and forgo doing other important activities to put up the walls and ultimately roof. The players are emotionally invested in the roof, so when it blows off it brings the players further into the story rather than just being seen as a random obstacle.

This is akin to the difference in the invocation of the endowment effect between receiving tokens, which do not trigger it, and objects like mugs and candy bars, which do. The abstract nature of the HUB, which is represented in the game by a large control panel, is too abstract to engage the player. So when it breaks down, it is an annoyance rather than a tragedy.

Another related complaint is that the constant malfunctioning is thematically dissonant. In Crusoe, the misfortunes that befall you are consonant with the theme and setting: storms batter your shelter, wild animals attack, players become injured and may develop gangrene. They fit with the fantasy of being stranded on a deserted island. The constant parade of HUB malfunctions in Martians does not fit the fantasy. Sometimes it seems like the players have been sent to Mars in a ramshackle bucket of bolts rather than the pinnacle of a worldwide effort to put humans on the surface of another planet.

A review of the game captures this nicely:

> The problem with First Martians is that it simply doesn't have this [NASA mission] feel of clockwork precision followed by knife-edge allocation of resources in case of a crisis. Instead, the game feels more strongly of constant improvisation—where little bad things keep happening and you're trying to fix them with the most minimal band-aid possible.[13]

The losses in Crusoe engage and challenge the player because the players have invested time and actions into their creation, and the losses fit the world. The losses in Martians, in contrast, seem arbitrary and out of place and punishing for the sake of giving the players obstacles to overcome.

Permadeath

In chapter 1, we discussed losing character levels and the negative feelings that can engender. The game *Diablo* was held up as an example of a game that does not include monsters or traps that eliminate items, levels, or abilities.

Diablo II did, however, add a mode called *hardcore*. If you play in hardcore mode, when your character dies, the game ends and the character is gone (although it may be enshrined in the Hall of Heroes, where you can view the character's last incarnation).

Hardcore mode, however, is initially locked. In *Diablo 2*, you needed to complete the game once before it was unlocked. In *Diablo 3*, that restriction was softened somewhat and you needed to reach level 10 with a normal character before the game would allow you to create a hardcore character. The developers expressed concern that new players would create hardcore characters without understanding the game and what hardcore really meant—leading to a negative game experience.

The permanent loss of a character is called *permadeath*. The concept of permadeath in a computer game goes back to *Rogue*.[14] In *Rogue*, you explored a dungeon, attempting to retrieve the amulet located on the bottom level. When your character died, the game ended. There was no save system, so you needed to succeed from start to finish without dying. Due to the length of the game, players wanted a save game feature added, and eventually the authors relented. However, players began to use it to reload repeatedly to win the game. This was against the design intent, and the developers stripped out the save feature. This style of permadeath is more akin to losing the game, rather than loss aversion in the sense that we are discussing, although there are of course parallels in raising the emotional stakes.

Let's turn our attention to the *X-COM*[15] and *Fire Emblem*[16] series of games. In these, you control a party of characters, and it is possible (likely, in fact) for characters to die. However, their death does not prevent you from finishing the game. In *X-COM*, for example, you recruit a new character to your team if one dies.

X-COM does allow you to restore to a saved state before a mission to permit you to avoid the character death. Most versions of *Fire Emblem* did not have this feature. If a character died, you either had to carry on or reset the game back to the beginning. Twenty years and twelve installments later, *Fire Emblem: New*

Mystery of the Emblem introduced "casual mode," which brought killed characters back to life at the end of a battle.

Permadeath is a central mechanic in *Fire Emblem*. The developers personalize the characters to create emotional attachments. Characters in the game have relationships with each other, get married, and have children. This dramatically increases the stakes as players make decisions and progress through the dangers of the game.

A post on Kotaku[17] spawned a lengthy discussion in the comment section about permadeath in *Fire Emblem*: "It's not *Fire Emblem* without Permadeath. I'm sorry it just isn't. That is why you have such colorful characters and the Support System, to feel bad when they die. Turning off Permadeath undermines the entire point of the Support System. It isn't about a game just being challenging. This isn't about whose [sic] the bigger gaming badass. It's about an entire mechanic of the game having meaning by keeping Permadeath on. Without it, the Support System is just a dating sim." Another user responds: "Well, a bunch of people just want to have fun while playing and I guess that 'feeling bad' isn't fun." The initial poster replies: "So you never watch any serious drama movies, tv, or books? Deaths have emotional impact and they make the story more memorable, AND they make you play better and smarter when each decision matters. I guess that is my point. If you play with Permadeath off, then you might as well just download some dating sims from Steam. You are only getting half a game."

Games, however, can differ in a key way from books and movies: the narrative outcome may not be predetermined. Yes, the death of beloved characters occurs in books and movies. But the event is not under the control of the reader or viewer; it will happen the same way every time. No matter how many times you read *Harry Potter and the Half-Blood Prince*, Dumbledore will die. Games can be different. In *Fire Emblem* and *X-COM*, the outcome of the battle is not preordained. Characters are living and dying because of the choices *you* make. There is always the thought that if you had done something differently, if you had made different decisions, if the random number generator had been different, the outcome would have been different. This is at the heart of loss aversion. It feels bad to lose something that you are attached to, that you feel endowed with. It feels much worse when your own decision leads to that loss.

Again, the point is not that invoking this type of loss is a bad thing to do in a game. *Fire Emblem* has been a very successful series. But designers need to understand that permadeath will alter the way players approach the game, and they need to carefully consider the way it is implemented and the options that players have. Designers need to enter the process of game development with their eyes open.

The idea that death can be avoided in a game if you just do the right thing is thoroughly ingrained in players. When a beloved character dies, it often sends players on a usually fruitless quest to replay the game and try to save them. For example, in *Final Fantasy VII*,[18] the death of the character Aeris comes as a huge shock to the player. Almost immediately after the release of the game, players began searching for a way to avoid her death. Urban legends began to sprout up about what players could do to avoid losing her.

The game *Hate Plus* has the players exploring an abandoned generation ship by communicating with two AI personalities. The *Mute AI was the head of security and *Hate Plus* tells the devastating story of how she loses hope and ultimately commits suicide at the end of the game rather than leave the ship. The designer subverts the concept of achievements and permadeath by including a Steam achievement called *Level Four Revive Materia* that was awarded if the player completed the game with *Mute still alive—except that there was no way to accomplish this. The designer has confirmed this many times, and yet players have continued to try to find a way to save her. Ultimately, these attempts resulted in a project to modify the game itself to allow the players to save *Mute before winning the game.

One person justified the effort this way: "Now *Hate Plus* is a great game, don't get me wrong, but there are some (not me) that feel their money was wasted because of the inability of helping *Mute. With this mod, people who felt that way can completely enjoy the game again, which already had two other great endings."

Designer Christine Love is not sure how to feel about these efforts:

> A consistent thread between *Analogue* and *Hate Plus* is that over the course of the two games, *Mute never has a shred of agency of her own, leaving every decision that affects her life in the player's hands…then players make a mod to rob her of the single piece of agency she has, to stop her during the one time she does get to act on her own beliefs.
>
> I'm happy people care about *Mute so much, but it just feels like the point was missed entirely? I don't know. I'm incredibly conflicted on the matter.[19]

Loss can have a powerful effect on players, especially losing something or someone that they considered theirs, or on their team, or even a friend.

3 Framing

Disease

When performing their original studies on loss aversion, Kahneman and Tversky did not just ask questions about money. They also tested people's reactions to different types of emotional and nonemotional stimuli.

Here's another set of choices they posed to subjects:

A deadly disease is rapidly spreading! If nothing is done, six hundred people will die.

You are the leader of the Pandemic Response Team and are presented with two options:

Option A	Two hundred people will be saved.
Option B	One in three chance that all six hundred are saved. Two in three chance that no people are saved.

When presented with these choices, 72 percent chose A—guaranteeing saving the lives of two hundred people.

Here's another set of options:

A deadly disease is rapidly spreading! If nothing is done, six hundred people will die.

You are the leader of the Pandemic Response Team and are presented with two options:

| Option C | Four hundred people will die. |
| Option D | One in three chance that no one dies. Two in three chance that six hundred die. |

What would your choice be? When presented with these options, 78 percent of people choose D.

I'm guessing that you see where we're going with this.

Choice A and choice C are exactly the same, as are choices B and D.

Take a look at it again:

Option A	Two hundred people will be saved.
Option B	One in three chance that all six hundred are saved. Two in three chance that no people are saved.
Option C	Four hundred people will die.
Option D	One in three chance that no one dies. Two in three chance that six hundred die.

With six hundred lives on the line, "two hundred people will be saved" is the same as "four hundred people will die." And a "two in three chance no people are saved" is equivalent to a "two in three chance that six hundred die." However, people react to these very differently. This is called the *framing effect*. The way that choices are presented can have a dramatic impact on how people answer.

One person I showed this to realized what the trick was, but she still couldn't bring herself to pick choice C—even though she had already picked choice A. "How can you pick a choice that says four hundred people die?" she said.

These results map very neatly onto the monetary loss aversion rules that we explored earlier. Two of the key findings are as follows:

- People will take a sure gain rather than gamble for a larger gain.
- People will gamble to avoid a sure loss.

And that is exactly what is happening here. In the first example, the choices are all expressed as gains, in a positive sense: two hundred people will be saved, or a two in three chance that no one is saved. *Saved* has a very positive connotation. Accepting the sure thing of A appeals to us more than the chance that no one is saved. And, conversely, when expressed as losses, or people dying, the sure loss is not as appealing as taking a chance to avoid losing people.

Manipulating framing is seen constantly in the world of sales and marketing. As a simple example, in California, Colorado, and several other US states, it was made illegal to charge a surcharge to a customer paying by credit card. It was, however, legal to give a discount for paying cash. The results were predictable. Merchants increased their prices slightly and offered discounts for cash. The same exact prices are paid as were paid before (with the credit card surcharges), but people and lawmakers felt better about it. It's more palatable for some people to receive a discount than for some to get a surcharge, even if the actual dollars changing hands are the same.

When laws regarding surcharges versus discounts were being debated before the US Senate Banking Committee in 1975, Jeffrey Bucher from the Federal Reserve Board maintained that there should be no distinction between discounts and surcharges—that they should be treated equally under the law. He did note, though, that "critics argued that a surcharge carries the connotation of a penalty on credit card users while a discount is viewed as a bonus to cash customers. They contended that this difference in psychological impact makes it more likely that surcharge systems will discourage customers from using credit cards."

Offsets and Isolation

Framing can be a highly effective way of affecting player emotion during game play. There are a variety of ways that it can be integrated into different mechanics, but perhaps the simplest is achieved simply by adding an offset to the gains and losses.

For example, here's a game:

You are given $1,000. Then you are asked to choose between:	
Option A	A 50 percent chance of winning $1,000.
Option B	A guaranteed $500.

As you should predict by now, 84 percent of people chose option B. Here's another game:

You are given $2,000. Then you are asked to choose between:	
Option C	A 50 percent chance of losing $1,000.
Option D	You must lose $500.

This time, 70 percent of people chose C.

Contrast this with the first two games we looked at in chapter 1:

Option E	An 80 percent chance of winning $4,000.
Option F	A 100 percent chance of winning $3,000.
Option G	An 80 percent chance of *losing* $4,000.
Option H	A 100 percent chance of *losing* $3,000.

Unlike the games from chapter 1, the new games (choices A–D) are *exactly* the same. In both options A and C, you have a 50 percent chance of ending with $1,000 and a 50 percent chance of ending with $2,000. In options B and D, you have a 100 percent chance of ending with $1,500.

However, by changing the framing—by offsetting the initial conditions of how much money you start with—the designer of these questions was able to express the first question in terms of gains and the second in terms of losses. In the first example, you are given $1,000 and can gain. In the second, you are given more money—$2,000—but can lose. And the natural inclination to want guaranteed gains, and to gamble to avoid losses, asserts itself.

Rather than simply switching terminology for losses and gains, this effect can be exploited by dividing a decision up into smaller decisions, a process called *isolation*. For example, people were asked to decide between these two choices:

Option A	A 20 percent chance of winning $4,000.
Option B	A 25 percent chance of winning $3,000.

Sixty-six percent said they would pick choice A—which is actually the correct option mathematically. Expectation value for

A is $800, and for B it is $750. Regardless of the math, this is in line with studies that show that people basically treat 20 percent and 25 percent as the same chances, which drives the selection of A, which has the higher dollar value.

Now let's look at another game:

This is a two-stage game. In the first stage, you have a 75 percent chance to simply lose the game and a 25 percent chance to move to the second round.

If you advance to the second round, you have a choice:

| Option C | An 80 percent chance of winning $4,000. |
| Option D | A 100 percent chance of winning $3,000. |

People were asked to choose either C or D *before* they knew if they were going to advance to the second round. In this case, 78 percent of people chose option D.

Mathematically, these two problems are *exactly* the same. Choice A in the first game and choice C in the second game are identical.[1] Remember, in the first game, 66 percent of people chose the $4,000 option, and in the second 78 percent chose the $3,000 option. Unlike our first loss aversion questions in chapter 1, in which the first game was gaining money and the second losing, the payouts on these two games are the same.

The point here isn't that people are bad at math. Well, in a way it is, but the important factor is that people rely on rules of thumb or gut feelings to make these decisions. In this and similar cases, people ignore the portion of the problem that overlaps. Because it applies to both choices, it can simply be factored out and ignored. Creating the first stage returns choices C and

D to one of our original loss aversion questions. Specifically, the reintroduction of the word *guaranteed* has a huge impact on people. This problem was specifically partitioned to give people a guaranteed pick with choice D, which they predictably flocked to. As we discussed in the first chapter, people give much more weight to choices that have a 100 percent chance of happening.

An *offset* manipulates the payout values, whereas *isolation* manipulates the payout probabilities. The effect of both is to make it more likely that people will select a certain option or perceive the option in a certain way. Poker has certain elements of this feature: players may treat the pot as an abstract, common pool of chips and overvalue their current bet. Sophisticated poker players lean heavily on the concept of *pot odds*, which explicitly links the immediate bet decision with the full mathematical picture.

Framing in Board Games

I ran into the phenomenon of framing with one of my tabletop game designs. In Pit Crew,[2] players play on teams and try to get their race car back out onto the track quickly while making as few mistakes as possible. When teams do good things, like getting out onto the racetrack first, their score marker moves up on a track. After three rounds, the team that has moved furthest along the scoring track is the winner. As mentioned, teams may make mistakes in fixing their car, either accidentally or intentionally, to get out faster. Those mistakes generate penalty points. The question we needed to resolve was this: What should those penalty points do?

We tested it two different ways. In the first iteration, penalty points moved you backward on the score track (see figure 3.1). In essence, penalty points were a negative score.

Figure 3.1
Pit Crew scoring track.

We also tested with several groups a setup in which penalty points, rather than moving your score marker backward, moved all the *other* score markers that number of spaces forward. So if your team got two penalty points, all the opposing teams moved forward two spaces.

From a game effect standpoint, this is exactly the same. Subtracting points from one team is the exact same thing as adding points to all the other teams.

The groups that played with the second system enjoyed the game much more. They tended to play with more abandon and were more willing to accept penalties to finish early and gain finishing bonuses. The groups that moved backward on the scoring track were much more concerned about the penalties. They did not want to move backward on the track and geared their play to avoid that happening, even if it hurt their overall position.

When we discussed both options with some of the groups, the sentiment was overwhelmingly in favor of the system in which penalty points moved your opponents forward. You always kept progress you had made. It was much less emotional to give a boost to your opponents than to have to give something back. For a family game, young gamers were also much more attracted to the "positive" system than the "negative" system.

The impact of framing is clear here. When the system is set up around gains, and somebody gains regardless of what happens, it makes for a more enjoyable experience, especially for casual and younger players. When you actually move backward for mistakes, it distorts the way players approach the game and makes for more infighting within the team if someone messes up. A happy bonus is that advancing on a track fits very well with the theme and metaphor of racing.

Around the same time that I was working on Pit Crew, I was developing another game that faced a similar choice: The Expanse,[3] based on a television series (see figure 3.2). In this game, players represent factions trying to spread influence and power throughout the solar system. They win by having the most control points (CP) at the end of the game. At certain points, I wanted players to have to spend CP to be able to do certain things—spend CP now in the hopes of a bigger reward later.

I seriously considered the option of having the other players gain CP in these cases instead of the acting player losing them, for similar reasons as in Pit Crew. It would have less emotional weight and make the players more comfortable. But The Expanse is a much heavier game than Pit Crew, and not really light-hearted or aimed at families. And while in Pit Crew I wanted to encourage players to play fast and loose with making mistakes, intentional

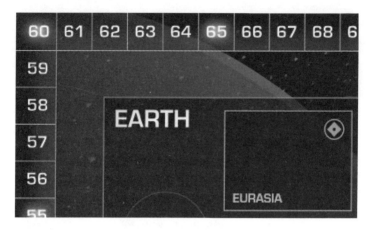

Figure 3.2
A portion of the scoring track in The Expanse.

or not, in The Expanse I wanted the decision to give up CP to feel emotional. I wanted the players to feel more invested in those decisions—to make it a bit more agonizing and difficult for players to make that choice. So in this case, to emphasize that difficult choice, I chose to force players to lose CP.

There are certainly many other games in which moving backward (more properly "getting sent back") is a key part. This is a feature of games ancient and modern, beginning with the five-thousand-year-old Egyptian game senet, through backgammon, pachisi, snakes and ladders, and, in a more modern incarnation, Sorry![4]

Over the last thirty years of game development, however, this reliance on punishing other players has diminished. As an example, the prototypical conquest game of the last century is Risk.[5] In this game, players battle over territories across the globe. However, it is essentially a zero-sum game. All the territories begin the game controlled by players, and the only way to progress in the game is to eliminate all the other players from the board. Games like this, with player elimination as the goal, including Monopoly,[6] have been the cause of many bad feelings during family game nights. This design methodology led to a certain marginalization of tabletop games through the mid-twentieth century.

Many games of this time, like Monopoly and Risk, follow a similar pattern. Players start with few or disconnected resources, build up better positions and gain stuff, and then have that position or their stuff destroyed. In Monopoly, this dynamic is expressed as starting with money but no properties. Players accumulate properties, build houses and hotels, and elevate their position. However, for all players except the winner, there is a turning point where the houses, hotels, properties, and money are all lost. Similarly, in Risk, players start with a few armies scattered all over the world. Gradually they build their forces and form perimeters to take and hold continents. However, again, for all except the winner, every army you have is going to be destroyed and every territory you control lost.

As we've demonstrated, via loss aversion and the endowment effect, getting things and then losing them is an emotional trigger point. Games that are set up like this engender a strong response and often lead to arguments and bad feelings.[7] This trend was turned around by the European school of game design—particularly in Germany, where the emphasis shifted away from winning through elimination to winning by advancing fastest, almost a race condition. A key turning point using this design methodology was the publication of the tabletop game the Settlers of Catan[8] (now simply called Catan), designed by Klaus Teuber. Catan offers several innovations, and we will

Figure 3.3
Settlements, cities, and roads in the Settlers of Catan.

revisit them in later chapters, but at this time I would like to focus simply on the victory condition. The theme of Catan is set- tling an uninhabited territory. The goal is not to gain dominance by eliminating or attacking the other players. It is to be the first player to reach ten points by building settlements and cities and achieving certain goals (see figure 3.3).

Settlements and cities allow players to gain more resources, as well as victory points. Importantly, these structures are perma- nent. They can never be lost. Although their effectiveness can be reduced by a robber mechanism, this can affect multiple players and is only temporary. Even so, a video from game review site the Dice Tower had the three hosts name their top ten most annoying board game characters. Two of the three included the Catan robber on their lists.[9]

There are only two ways that points can be earned in Catan, and subsequently taken away: having the largest army, which is represented by soldier cards, and having the longest road. However, you lose these points only by another player getting more soldier cards or a longer road than you have. There is no way to "attack" another player's army to reduce its size. You simply have to build yours up to be larger.[10]

Although only one player is the winner at the end of a game of Catan, all players will end up with more than what they started with. This shift to emphasize growth rather than destruction became the hallmark of the European game design aesthetic.

Modern games that build on the theme of Risk (games of conquest) have embraced this as well. Although there is destruction, as these are conflict games, it is not about ultimate destruction. Nexus Ops,[11] Kemet,[12] Eclipse,[13] and Cry Havoc[14] are all about attacking and growing more powerful than your opponents, and all involve the collection of points to win the game rather than wiping other players off the map.

Nexus Ops is probably the clearest Risk descendent, both in the way it plays and its publisher (Hasbro). Via cards, it assigns missions to players to take certain territories or win battles under certain conditions to gain points. Winning battles also awards points. The other games work in a similar fashion. Points are awarded for territory, technology, and other factors, in addition to battles. Attacking players is a means to an end but not the objective, and players cannot be eliminated from the game. All of this leads to a less emotionally fraught conflict game in which players always have the opportunity to avenge a lost battle.

Framing in Video Games

This sensibility has been embraced in the video game world as well, although video games often combine destruction with increasing power by all players. To go back to our original board game examples, Risk and Monopoly, when you lose stuff you also lose the things that allow you to achieve victory. For example, in Monopoly, when you lose money to other players or have to sell off houses or hotels, you are losing the very tools that you need to achieve victory. In Risk, the loss of territories and armies makes it harder to conquer your opponents. Risk does have the "card set" mechanic via which you can gain bonuses that increase in value, but this is a patch to cover up a system with a strong negative feedback loop.

Modern video games typically incorporate destruction on a separate "track" that doesn't directly penalize the team. For example, in *League of Legends*, two teams of players battle to destroy their opponents' Nexus. The first team to destroy the Nexus is victorious. To destroy the Nexus, teams must also destroy towers and inhibitors, which are defensive structures. However, the loss of these structures doesn't penalize the team that lost them. Either the effect is neutral, or it gives a bonus to the opposing team. All teams in *League of Legends* end the game more powerful than when they started.

There are several connected parameters in *League of Legends*. Each player chooses a champion they will play during the game. That champion starts with few abilities and is fairly weak. Computer-controlled minions are spawned at regular intervals, and by defeating those minions, champions earn gold and experience. Experience can be used to gain levels, increasing strength and allowing for improvement of each champion's special attacks, eventually unlocking their ultimate ability at level 6. Gold is used to purchase items, like swords, armor, or potions, that give bonuses and special abilities.

So what happens when a champion is killed? Are they permanently out of the game? Do they lose gold or experience, or reset back to level 1? None of these. The champion is out of the match for a few seconds (the exact time depending on how far into the match it is) and then respawns exactly as it was, with full health and mana. While waiting to respawn, players can purchase additional items from the shop, so even that wait time is mitigated somewhat.

Although being out of the match for a few seconds (plus the time required to walk back to the front lines) can be critical in a close match, Riot has positioned the other effects in a positive frame rather than a negative one—as bonuses instead of penalties. If a champion dies, the player who landed the killing blow earns an experience and gold boost. This allows for better abilities and items and makes the team more powerful. However, it does not penalize the champion who was killed.

In essence, *League of Legends* is positioned as a race game. The teams never move backward. When you complete a game, whether you have won or lost, you always end up more powerful than when you started. This parallels the core gameplay of Catan, in which you end up better than you started, win or lose. So players experience the game in a positive way, even if they lose. They will get to unlock better abilities and explore different item combinations regardless of how the game goes. They do not find themselves in a death spiral of decreasing ability or resources. They may have fewer resources than their opponents, but they always have more relative to their starting position. Even if players do absolutely nothing in *League of Legends*, the champions constantly accumulate gold. This is an economy of abundance in the midst of destruction.

The game *Dota 2*,[15] a competitor of *League of Legends*, does penalize players directly for deaths. When a champion is killed, the opposing team gains gold and experience (as in *League of Legends*), but the defeated champion also loses gold. In comparisons between the games, this is specifically highlighted as a feature that is more "punishing" for the players and makes the games less "accessible."[16] Although there are many features in *Dota 2* that lead to its reputation as a more complex, demanding game, the loss of gold upon death gives the game a more ruthless reputation.

This could be modified by shifting the framing. Eliminating the gold loss to the champion who was killed and increasing the gold gained by the team that scored the kill could sidestep this problem. But one advantage of the current system is that it adds a push-your-luck element because once gold is spent on items, they are yours to keep. Players need to balance the loss of time spent going back to base to cash in their gold with the risk of losing it if killed. Again, the purpose of this discussion of framing and loss aversion is not to say that one way is right and another wrong. It is to understand the emotional impact of game design decisions.

As mentioned earlier, early twentieth-century tabletop games like Monopoly and Risk followed a pattern of growth and building up, followed by destruction. In video games, there are many games that follow this pattern—one of the most famous being *Starcraft*.[17] In *Starcraft*, each player begins with a base that produces minerals, which can be used to create basic units or buildings—which, in turn, can be used to produce more advanced units. The goal of the game is the complete destruction of the other player's base.

Starcraft has phases similar to those in Monopoly or Risk— an early growth period, during which players develop their strategies, marked by small clashes, followed by larger and larger skirmishes until one side is destroyed. There is absolutely no positive framing in *Starcraft*. As your buildings get destroyed, you lose your ability to build new units to counter the next attack. If your mineral-gathering units are destroyed, it can set you back quite a lot because you will fall behind on building new units. It is very much an unstable equilibrium: a small advantage snowballs into something larger and larger.

In addition, only the winner emerges with a base. The other players all end in destruction, their buildings in ruins. Although it is possible to win the game simply by destroying the enemy headquarters and not necessarily all of their production buildings, destroying the infrastructure of the opponent is typically a key prerequisite to victory.

One of the most popular streaming and eSports games is *Counter Strike: Global Offensive* (*CS:GO*).[18] *CS:GO* is a multiplayer, team-based shooter played over a series of short rounds. At the start of a round, each player gets money to spend on weapons and equipment. Players start with a base of $800 and get additional funds based on what they did the previous round. Scoring kills and achieving objectives give a player additional money in the next round. Although the penalty for death is fairly steep in the short term—being eliminated from that round of play—it does not affect the player monetarily for the next round.

On the other hand, there are some negative monetary penalties that can be applied to the players. In some missions, one team is trying to rescue hostages. Shooting hostages results in loss of funds for the next round. Shooting teammates (friendly fire) also results in lost funds for the next round. In this case, the designers are using loss aversion to their advantage by disincentivizing the players from performing activities that are inarguably bad within the context of the game. Friendly fire, in particular, fits with the type of shooter that *CS:GO* presents—one that focuses on stealth, positioning, and realism. In contrast, other shooters such as *Overwatch*[19] do not include friendly fire effects, keeping in line with the cartoonish play style and casual audience.

In terms of framing, the money system in *CS:GO* is reminiscent of gold in *League of Legends*. Both are gained (to a limited extent) even if you do nothing. Both are awarded for doing good things in the game and allow your character to become more powerful. And both express competition not by having one team take gold away from the other team (or take more from a central pot than the other team) but by having a winning team accruing it at a faster rate, which the team needs to parlay into an on-field advantage.

There is also a broad swath of games that have what can be termed a *neutral* framing. The abilities of the players remain relatively constant throughout the game. Blizzard's shooter *Overwatch* falls into this category. In *Overwatch*, there is no character progression. The abilities you start with are the abilities you have throughout the game. You can earn an "ultimate" ability by "charging" it through various activities. Once the ultimate is used, the charging resets back to zero, and the player must charge it up again. But death does not affect this in any way. If you die with your ultimate 80 percent charged, you return a few seconds later with your ultimate still 80 percent charged. Other than time out of the game, there are no negative penalties to abilities or character strength.

In the video game arena, games like *Starcraft* have been declining in popularity and have been usurped by multiplayer online battle arena (MOBA) games and other team games, as well as battle royale games.[20] In 2015, MOBAs accounted for 58 percent of watched eSports hours on the streaming service Twitch. Shooters like *CS:GO* accounted for 27 percent and strategy games like *Starcraft* for only 10 percent.[21]

Although there is no data suggesting causation, the trend is toward games that use positive framing, emphasizing growth rather than destruction. Battle royale games like *Fortnite*[22] are an interesting contrast, as we'll discuss in chapter 6. And as we saw in our discussion of the Tracking card in *Hearthstone* in chapter 1, restructuring the way the actions of the player are described can preserve the game impact while changing the approach the player takes. Changing this:

> **Look at the top three cards of your deck. Draw one and discard the others.**

to this:

> **Look at the top three cards of your deck. Keep one and shuffle the other two back into your deck. Then discard the bottom two cards in your deck without looking at them.**

changes the entire psychology of the player actions.

The key lesson is that game systems can be designed and presented to the players in different ways. Adding or removing the same quantity from all decisions, or from all players, can make a big difference in the decisions that are made and the experience that players have.

4 Utility Theory

One of the key elements of loss aversion is understanding how people value things. In previous chapters, we examined how ownership may alter value through the endowment effect and how using emotionally loaded language may impact perception through framing.

In this chapter, we take a closer look at another element of value: how much use, or *utility*, you believe you may get out of something.

Deal or No Deal

The premise of the television game show *Deal or No Deal*[1] is straightforward: You are shown twenty-six identical briefcases, each of which is secretly worth a different amount of money ranging, in the US version, from $1 to $1 million. You select one case, and it is set aside. Then you select other cases to be opened, revealing how much they contained. You are hoping for low values, making it more likely the case you selected has a high value. After opening a certain number of cases (depending on the round), the "banker" makes you an offer for your case. You need to look at the possible values that can still be in your case, and then you need to decide if you want to take the offer or keep going and open another case.

For example, let's say there are three cases left to be opened, so four cases including yours. The possible values remaining are $1, $10,000, $250,000, and $1 million. The banker offers to give you $150,000 for your case. If you accept, the game ends, and you get the money. If not, you need to open another case, and you'll get a new offer from the banker. If you open the $1 case, eliminating that value from possibly being in your case, your offer will go up, probably by a lot. But if you eliminate the $1 million case, your offer will go way down.

What would you do? Watching people wrestle with this decision is the heart of the show.

Once I was with a big group watching *Deal or No Deal.* To everyone's annoyance, I pointed out that there was a simple mathematical answer as to whether you should accept or reject the offer: Determine the average value of the possible values and compare it to the offer. If the offer is lower than the average value, reject it. If not, take it. In the preceding example, the offer for $150,000 is less than the average of the four cases, which is a shade above $300,000. So you should reject the offer.

The group I was watching with will no longer watch game shows with me. Watching games with game designers is always perilous, as they like to strip away the magic and expose the bones. In this case, while I was mathematically correct, I neglected to take economics and psychology into account.

As a game designer, I was defining *winning* as walking away with the highest possible amount of money. Based on that criteria, my analysis was spot on. The average amount of money left in the game is called, in probability theory, the *expectation value*, or *EV.* The EV is the amount of money you would expect to have, on average, if you play the game over and over again from that position.

If you start calculating the amount the banker offers and the average value of the remaining cases, you'll see that in *Deal or No Deal* the offer is always less than the average. It is much less than the average early in the game as a way of encouraging players to keep playing, and it gradually gets closer to the average later in the game. But it almost never exceeds the average value. So, strictly from the perspective of maximizing your winnings, you should never take the offer.

But people do, of course. Are they making a mistake? From a pure math perspective, yes. But the wrinkle is that people define *winning* differently. Maximizing your winnings may not be the definition that everyone uses, particularly when large amounts of money are involved.

Let's look at a very simple example. There are two cases left: $1 and $1 million. The average value of these cases is $500,000. The banker offers $400,000. Do you take this offer?

Most people would, even though they are, from the pure math standpoint, leaving $100,000 on the table (the difference between the offer and the average value). One reason for this is what is called the *utility* of the money, as described by utility theory. *Utility theory* describes how desirable something is. This can be very difficult to describe in absolute terms and varies wildly from person to person. Is $1 million twice as desirable as $500,000? It depends on who you are and what your situation is.

If you're running a huge corporation, making $1 million on a deal is twice as good as making $500,000. But if you're a normal middle-class person, there's not that much difference between getting a check for $500,000 and getting one for $1 million. Both amounts will change your life. Research in utility theory shows this. As monetary values become very large, the desirability curve flattens. We make very little distinction between $3 billion and $4 billion. Going back to our original loss aversion formation, here is another choice:

Option A	A 99.9 percent chance of winning $4 billion and a 0.1 percent chance of winning nothing.
Option B	A 100 percent chance of winning $3 billion.

Almost everyone is going to take choice B. From a purely mathematical standpoint, choice A is worth an extra *billion* dollars—but I can't imagine that anyone would take choice A on the one-in-a-thousand chance that they end up with nothing.

From a utility theory perspective, for almost anyone, $3 billion and $4 billion are exactly the same amount of money. So, no matter how high the chance of getting the $4 billion, so long as it's not 100 percent, very few people will take that chance.

Path Dependence

Deal or No Deal nicely illustrates another effect that needs to be considered in interpreting player actions.

A 2008 study of over 150 games of *Deal or No Deal* broadcast in the Netherlands, Germany, and the United States showed that the risk people were willing to take was strongly influenced by how the course of the game went. If the game started going poorly for the player, and they eliminated many high prize possibilities, their loss aversion went down. They were much more aggressive in rejecting bank offers, even as they approached or even exceed the expectation value.

One example cited in the paper was about a contestant on the Dutch show, named Frank. At round 6, the remaining possible prizes for Frank were €0.5, €10, €100, €10,000, and €500,000. The average of these is €102,000, and the bank offered €75,000, which Frank rejected.

The next case Frank opened was the highest: €500,000. The average dropped to €2,500, and the bank offered €2,400, almost equal to the average, which again was rejected.

Frank continued to reject offers until he was faced with the final two cases—one containing €10 and one containing €10,000. The bank offered €6,000, which is well above the average of €5,000. Here, the math, loss aversion, and utility theory all agreed: Frank should take the offer.

However, he rejected it and ended up with only €10.

Although this is an extreme case in the study's examples, the data clearly shows that players who suffered big losses were much less likely to accept deals as they pushed to recover what they considered to be their lost money—even though it wasn't theirs to begin with. It was just virtual and "on paper." This is evocative of our examination of framing in the prior chapter. In Frank's case, he didn't see the €6,000 offer versus the €5,000 expected value. In his mind, he had lost the €75,000 offer, so he was willing to gamble to minimize that loss.

Remember our general rules about loss aversion: people will take a sure gain over a gamble for a bigger gain, and they will gamble to avoid a loss. Frank's perspective was that he had suffered a loss, even though he hadn't paid to play the game or lost any actual money. When people suffer losses, it makes them more willing to take bigger risks. In poker, this behavior is well-known and is called going *on tilt*. Players who are on tilt take bigger chances and don't use proper strategy.

Endowment Effect

A quick aside before we leave *Deal or No Deal*. The first thing a player does in the game is select a case, and it is brought down to the front of the stage and placed on a table next to the player under a spotlight.

Why do this? It's not necessary for the mechanism of the game. It could very easily be designed so that the player doesn't select that initial case. The player could just start opening cases, and then after a few the banker could make an offer. Whether you select a case at the start, or just end up with a case after eliminating all the others makes no difference to the math of the situation.

The math may be the same, but the psychology of the two situations could not be more different. This is a genius bit of game design that leverages the endowment effect discussed in detail in chapter 2. Having the player select a case first, and physically moving it next to them, is such a simple thing. But it completely changes the feel of the game. That's YOUR case now, and all your hopes and dreams are with that numbered, shiny silver object.

Push-Your-Luck Games

In board games, there is a design mechanic called *push your luck*. A push-your-luck game presents the player with a decision of whether to end their turn with what they have now or to take another turn to try to improve their position at the risk of busting and losing everything.

There are many games that use this mechanic, including blackjack, Cosmic Wimpout,[2] farkel,[3] and Incan Gold,[4] but arguably one of the best is Sid Sackson's Can't Stop.[5] In Can't Stop, players try to advance up a series of tracks numbered 2–12 (see figure 4.1). On their turn, a player rolls four dice and splits them

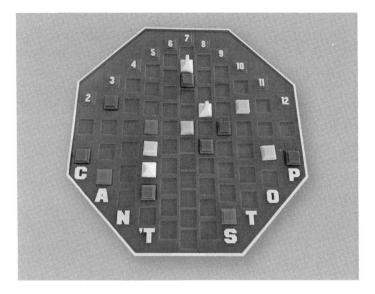

Figure 4.1
Can't Stop game in progress.

up into two pairs, as they choose. For example, if the dice are 2, 3, 3, 6, they could be divided as 5/9 or 6/8. They can then move a marker up on each of those columns, and these columns become "active" for the turn.

The player can then stop, ending their turn and locking in their progress, or they can roll again. However, only three columns can be active on any given turn. If a player rolls and can't make a combination that matches one of the three active columns, they bust and lose all progress made that turn.

For the game designer, the biggest advantage to a push-your-luck game is that it presents the player with only two choices: try again or walk away. There aren't hundreds of possible moves, like you might see in Go. The player's decisions are limited, and the consequences are clear. Such designs have a delightful way of immediately engaging the player, regardless of skill level or age. But these games also come with a strong emotional component. With a throw of the dice, you are risking everything that you gained this turn. Loss aversion plays a huge role in generating this emotion.

The fun and tricky part in Can't Stop is, as the name implies, when to stop your turn and lock in your progress. And this is where utility theory enters the mix. To peel back the layers a bit, let's look at a very simplistic version of Can't Stop. The rules are this:

> **Roll a die, and gain a (temporary) point if you roll a 1–5. If you roll a 6, you bust and lose any accumulated points.**

When should you roll, and when should you stop?

Let's take a small mathematical excursion. The math-phobic among you can skip down to the summary in bold. Obviously, with zero points, you should roll. After that, for each subsequent roll, you can calculate your *expectation value*. As we have seen before, this is what the average result would be over repeating the choice many, many times. To calculate it, you multiply the chance of something happening times your value if it happens. So, with one point, you have a 5/6 chance of gaining one point and a 1/6 chance of losing one point. Choosing to roll gives you $5/6*1 + 1/6*(-1)$, or 4/6 of a point gain. Because your expected gain is positive, you should roll.

If you have two points, your expectation value is $5/6*1 + 1/6*(-2)$, which is +3/6 of a point.

At five points, rolling gives an expectation value of zero. So rolling or not rolling gives you the same average result. Once you get to six points or more, on average you will lose points, so you should stop.

To summarize:

Once you get to five points, you should probably stop.

This is not a very interesting game at this point. There's a simple, mathematical go/no-go formula at each point in your turn to maximize your score. So, let's add a very small, and realistic, new rule: the first player to accumulate ten points wins the game. With this additional rule, the complexion of the decisions players have to make changes in a meaningful way.

Let's say you've got three points banked, and you've got six temporary points. If you stop now, you'll have nine points. Should you stop or roll? The math says you should stop. On average, you'll lose more than you gain. But that extra point will give you the victory, and so it's worth a lot more than a "regular" point. To use the language of utility theory, seven points have a lot more utility than six points in this situation.

To make that decision, you also want to look at where your opponents are. If none of them has more than one or two points, you're probably safe locking in at nine and trying to win on your next turn. But if someone is at eight or nine points, you almost certainly want to go for the win immediately because you probably won't have another chance.

Putting an end goal in the game immediately creates a utility landscape that constantly changes as the game state changes. Having a goal is key; without it, the game becomes a simple mathematical exercise, devoid of tension or decisions. The existence of a target (which may be a fixed endpoint or a target created by the status of the other players) creates a series of interesting decisions for the players, amplified by the emotional impact of loss aversion.

The Ten-Times Game

As a final example of utility theory, let's take a look at another game.

I put one dollar into a pot. You can either walk away and take the pot, or you can flip a coin and call heads or tails. If you're right, I'll multiply the money in the pot by ten. If you're wrong, you lose everything.

If you win, you have the same choice—walk away with your winnings or flip a coin again. But now the pot has ten dollars in it. So you can walk away with ten dollars or flip the coin for a chance to increase the pot to one hundred dollars.

Do you stop at $1? $10? $100? $1 million? When do you call it quits and walk away from the table and take the winnings?

What does math tell you to do? Our rule of thumb is that you should go with the choice that gives you the highest expectation value. With our simple die-rolling, push-your-luck game, the math told us that once we got to five points there was no reason to roll anymore. The math here is quite simple. Let's say we're at the ten-dollar level. We have a 50 percent chance of losing ten dollars, and a 50 percent chance of gaining ninety dollars (to a total of one hundred dollars). So:

$$(1/2 \times -10) + (1/2 \times 90) = 40$$

Our expectation value of flipping a coin is + forty dollars. Our expectation value of walking away with the pot is + ten dollars (because it's a sure thing). Therefore, math says we should flip the coin. The advantage to flipping is huge.

There's one small problem, though: no matter what level we're at, the math will always say that taking that bet is a good thing. Therefore, says math, you should never stop flipping the coin. But, of course, that means that eventually you will lose and end with nothing.

If you want to win, you have to walk away. And the decision about when to do that will vary based on your personal utility function.

So—when would *you* walk away?

5 Endowed Progress

It may seem like loss aversion creates negative emotions and leaves players as quivering husks of fear and doubt. However, using the right techniques can create a series of positive moments that build momentum and positive feeling—and propel players through the game.

Let's look at a nifty experiment that demonstrates this.

Car Wash Experiment

In 2004, researchers Joseph Nunes and Xavier Dreze conducted an experiment at a California car wash.[1] They handed out three hundred loyalty cards. Half of them needed eight stamps to earn a free car wash. The other half needed ten stamps, but two of the spots were already stamped. So, in both cases, eight additional stamps were required to earn the free wash. Then they sat back to see how many customers completed the cards.

Nineteen percent of the customers with the eight-stamp cards redeemed them for a free car wash. But 34 percent of those who had the ten-stamp cards redeemed theirs. Even though consumers had to return to the car wash an equal number of times, almost double the number of people who got the two free starter stamps completed the task.

Giving the consumers a head start made them much more likely to complete the task. The researchers called this the *endowed progress effect*. Giving progress to people made them more invested in the program. It made them think that they already had started the task and gave them a sense of commitment.

Endowed progress is yet another aspect of loss aversion. Nunes and Dreze chose the adjective *endowed* to show the relationship between this effect and the endowment effect discussed in chapter 2. The act of giving something to someone triggers a possessive, emotional response. For the Weighted Companion Cube, it made the players remember that they had to carry the cube through the level. In the car wash experiment, it made people feel like they had something to lose—and made them more likely to "finish the level," even if it was something as mundane as getting eight car washes.

Hearthstone Ranked Play

Sometimes games want to include systems that inherently involve gains and losses. Into these games, designers frequently will incorporate carefully considered features to blunt loss aversion by the players. One such example is *Hearthstone* ranked play.

In this system, players earn "stars" by winning games; as a result, they move up a ranking ladder. The winner of a match gains a star, and the defeated player loses a star. If you earn five stars, you move up a rank on the ladder. Higher numbered ranks are worse; the worst rank is 25. If you reach rank 1 and move beyond that, you gain Legendary rank and receive a number that represents your specific rank among the Legendary players.

There are a few interesting features that Blizzard has added to the *Hearthstone* ranking system that deserve examination in the context of loss aversion.

1. Low Ranks

At rank 20 or below (*below* means a worse rank—21–25 in this case), players do not lose stars. The winner gains a star, but the defeated player does not lose one. Players at these lower ranks are typically beginning *Hearthstone* players, a category of players that the designers want to encourage to stick with the game. By removing any consequence of losing, they get players comfortable with the ranking ladder and only reward victory. Defeat has no effect at all.

2. Win Streaks

Any time a player wins three games in a row, they gain two stars instead of one. Most players win around 50 percent of their games. Even the best players only win around 60 percent of games. The win streak bonus gives players who win half their games the ability to continue to move up the ladder. They will not hit a point of loss at which they see themselves slipping back down. In fact, a player can have as low a win rate as 46 percent and still, statistically, not lose ground on the ladder. This avoids discouraging players of lower ability. It keeps them involved in the game and gives them hope and opportunity for quick movement up the ladder.

Interestingly, this win streak bonus goes away when players reach rank 5 and better. And at the Legendary ranks, stars are no longer awarded: you simply move up and down ranks based on the level of the players you battle against.

3. Ranked Chests

When players achieve a rank, they are awarded a ranked chest of that level. At the end of the month (when the "ladder season" ends and ranks reset), players may open their chest and receive new cards and other in-game materials. The higher the rank you achieved, the better the chest. But even if you move down levels, the rank of your chest does not. It represents the high-water mark of your achievement for the season. For example, if you reach rank 8 but then lose several games and drop to rank 9, at the end of the season you will still receive the rank 8 chest.

These chests were a later addition to *Hearthstone*. At launch, the ranked play system merely gave bragging rights at the end of the season and were a way to judge your own play. This resulted in players having what became known as *ladder anxiety*. If you reached a good rank, perhaps better than any you'd achieved before (in fact, especially in this case), loss aversion would kick in and you wouldn't want to slip down. The fear of losing your rank overshadowed the positive feeling you would gain by achieving even higher ranks.

Ranked chests gave something tangible to gain from ladder play. And by marking their high-water rank, no matter what happens, players are given a specific reminder and representation—a souvenir, if you will—of their best performance.

4. Zero Levels

This is a subtle and interesting design choice. The top tier of one rank and the bottom tier of the rank above it are the same in game terms, but they are presented differently.

An example will help clarify this. At rank 13, you need to gain five stars to advance to level 12. When you have five stars, it is displayed as having all your stars filled in on rank 13. When you gain one more star, you advance to rank 12, and that star becomes your first star on rank 12. So you need to gain four more to fill up the stars and be ready to go to rank 11. But if you have one star at rank 12 and lose it, you do not go down to rank 13 with five stars—which is where you came from. Instead, it is displayed as zero stars on rank 12. Now if you lose another star, you go to rank 13 with four stars filled in. In other words, five stars at rank 13 is the same as zero stars at rank 12. You will see five stars at rank 13 on the way up the ladder, and zero stars on rank 12 on the way down the ladder.

This is a very subtle decision that can lead to some player confusion at first. So why include this feature? The answer is that it gives players an extra buffer before they lose a rank. Once you reach a rank, you must in essence lose two games, not just one, to move down a rank.

5. Starting Stars

At the beginning of each month, each player's rank resets back to the bottom of the ladder. However, you earn "starter stars" based on how you did the previous month—stars that almost all players earn (see figure 5.1). This is directly analogous to the car wash experiment previously discussed. Giving players stars immediately puts them on the road to advancement and is a strong motivating factor to continue playing the game.

The cumulative effect of these design decisions on a standard ladder system are all designed to get players to start and keep playing the game. They reduce or even eliminate the negative psychology of losing stars and ranks and focus players more on the upside potential than the chances of slipping back down the ladder.

Chess Rankings

Whereas short-term ladder systems don't try to seriously assess absolute skill levels, there are some that do.

One example is the system of chess ratings that are assigned in the United States by the US Chess Federation (USCF). Many

Figure 5.1
Bonus stars earned at the start of a *Hearthstone* season.

feel that these are absolute measurements of player skill, but in truth they measure relative ability (at best). Although the details of this system are outside the scope of this book, there is one feature I'd like to touch on.

Like all gamers, chess players have a tendency to obsess over their ratings. And through playing less—and simple loss of ability as we get older—ratings sometimes will drop. Because players tend to get upset when their ratings go down, the USCF has added a "rating floor" to its system.[2] Your rating can never, in your entire life, drop below your rating floor.

This helps people's egos, but it also further distorts the rating system and moves it away from its purpose: ratings that reflect skill levels.

Liquor Store Experiment

Before we get into the game design implications of endowed progress, let's take a quick look at another version of the car wash experiment that Nunes and Dreze reported on as part of their original paper.[3]

The researchers hypothesized that if you just gave someone a bonus, a head start, without any type of explanation about why you were doing so, people would be suspicious about your motivations and be less likely to cash it in.[4] This experiment was performed in a liquor store. Some customers were told that they needed to purchase a certain dollar value of liquor to receive a bonus bottle. Some people were just started on the program, whereas others were given a ten-dollar head start toward the goal. Of those who received the ten-dollar bonus, some were just given it, and others were given it along with an explanation about the store running a special promotion for an upcoming holiday.

Another group, instead of needing to achieve a certain dollar value, was awarded points with each bottle purchased. When reaching a point threshold, members of this group would earn a bonus bottle. Again, some people were given bonus points to start with, and others were not. And of those who received the bonus, some were given an explanation, and others were not.

The results were intriguing and only partially supported the suppositions of the researchers. When people received the monetary value as a starting bonus, the endowed progress effect only kicked in when they were given an explanation. Those who just got the starting purchases on their card did not feel the urge to complete the task. However, when the points system was used, the explanation had no effect. The endowment effect was triggered either way.

This underscores the effect we saw in the first chapter when we discussed casino games. The use of an artificial currency—points in this case, chips for the casino—puts people into a different head space than money does. People need to be separated from the value for many of these psychological effects to manifest. The value of money is too tangible.

The Settlers of Catan

Games frequently exploit endowed progress to keep players engaged. Let's return to the Settlers of Catan, introduced in chapter 3. The objective of the game is to be the first player to get to ten points. Points are mainly gained by building settlements (one point) or cities (two points). But players start with two settlements on the board—so they already begin the game with two points out of the ten required for victory.

This is exactly analogous to the car wash experiment. In the experiment, people received coupons that required ten stamps to win a free wash, and two were already punched. That almost doubled patrons' engagement with the promotion. In Catan, starting with ten stamps and needing two more has been replaced with needing ten points and starting with two.

And recall that most points in Catan, particularly those at the start and those gained by building other structures, can never be lost. These are permanent victory points that continually push players toward the win and the game toward a conclusion. The two ways of gaining temporary points—by having the longest road or the largest army—typically change hands through race conditions as another player creates a longer road or a bigger army. The roads and armies of other players are never directly attacked; these points are lost only if another player becomes the leader in these areas. This neatly sidesteps loss aversion in players because although you are losing the points gained from leading in these categories, you don't actually lose any in-game "stuff." It is a more abstract loss, and you always end the game with more stuff than you had when you started.

More modern conflict games that seek to fill the same niche as games like Risk have adopted similar approaches to winning the game. In Kemet, players build armies and attack each other, trying to take over territories on the board. However, whereas winning in Risk means taking everything away from the other players, in Kemet there are a variety of ways to gain victory points, including winning battles, taking temple spaces on the board, obtaining certain special cards, and more. And, like in Catan, players win by getting to ten points. Points in Kemet can be either permanent or temporary. Winning battles yields permanent points, while temple spaces give temporary victory points for as long as you hold them.

This balance of types of victory points has several positive effects on game play. First, players have a sense of forward progress. Permanent victory points mean that players are growing and advancing—and even if their armies are defeated and pushed back on the board, they have a permanent base of points to build on that can never be taken way.

Also, the game itself pushes toward a conclusion. Games in which one player needs to take over everything, like Risk, tend to be very long, as players fight back and forth over the same territory. Risk needed to include escalating set values that eventually give players overwhelming force to take over everything. The game also tends to require a "rich get richer" snowball effect as leaders get more resources to enable them to overcome the other players all banding against them. By having permanent victory points based on winning battles, Kemet ensures that the game will end in a reasonable time frame and will always be heading toward closure. The points ratchet up, and the end looms closer each turn.

Finally, having a mix of harder-to-gain permanent points and easier-to-gain temporary points gives an exciting dynamism to the game, which presents the players with choices about when to stretch for temporary points to try to win. It also adds a narrative arc to the game. As players accumulate more permanent points, the battles for temporary points take on increased importance—and players fight for them with greater desperation.

Catan was published almost ten years before the car wash experiment was performed. I don't believe that the experiment was based on Catan, but the parallels are eerie and intriguing. It is also unclear if having the players start with two points was a calculated move on the part of designer Klaus Teuber or if it was simply a happy accident resulting from the way the game needs to start and the scores such a start endows the players with.

Either way, those two starting points are arguably a key part of what immediately makes players feel invested; they give the impression that it won't take that much more to win the game—that the goal is tantalizingly close.

Experience in RPGs

Dungeons & Dragons enshrined the concept of characters gaining experience points to gain levels. With that innovation, it also created perhaps the most commonly used endowed progress effect in gaming.

Here's a typical chart showing a player's level when they gain a certain number of experience points:

Experience	Level
0	1
1,000	2
3,000	3
6,000	4
10,000	5

If a character has 1,200 experience points, they are level 2. Very rarely do players hit a level threshold exactly. Almost always, they overshoot the threshold and are already on the road toward the next level. This creates momentum because players are almost never at the beginning of the road to the next milestone. They are always a few steps along: probably not many, but enough to trigger the psychology of having started on a journey and being committed. There's no time to take a breath, as it were, at a level break and to ponder the long road to the next level. You are almost always endowed with some progress toward the next goal. This momentum carries players from goal to goal and maintains engagement. Over the years, this technique has been refined and incorporated across a variety of genres.

One improvement in game design has been shortening the distance between goals. Moving from level 9 to 10 in D&D can take quite a bit of in-game time. Designers have been shrinking this timeline, increasing the impact of having partially completed goals.

An excellent example of this can be seen in the computer game *Civilization*.[5] *Civilization* is a turn-based game, but the turns are very short—and, critically, the duration of most things you want to do requires multiple turns. For example, research projects may take ten turns to complete, a new building for your city may take eight turns, or moving a settler to found a city may take twelve turns. As you get more cities and grow your civilization, you have more and more of these projects running in parallel. But because they all end at different times, you always have some short-term goal that is in progress. Each of these goals in and of itself gives psychological impetus to the game. But having so many of them in different stages creates a compulsion, a palpable forward momentum that forces the player to continue on, turn after turn.

It's no surprise that *Civilization* earned a reputation for players spending marathon sessions playing it hour after hour, wanting to get in "just one more turn." The combination of short turns and staggered multiturn projects taps directly into the psychology of endowed progress to keep players engaged and wanting to bring things to completion.

Even though they are typically much shorter than RPGs or computer games like *Civilization*, board games have also been adopting these ideas. In general, turn structures have become shorter and more interleaved. It is rare to see a game like the war games of the 1970s and 1980s, in which one player would take an hour to perform their move while the other simply watched. Turns are much more bite-sized. Tactical games like PanzerBlitz,[6] in which each player took long turns while their tanks dashed from bush to bush, have now been replaced by games like Combat Commander[7] and Infinity.[8] These newer games have activation systems where movement distances are short, destinations can rarely be reached in one turn, and opponents have ample opportunity to react to partially hatched schemes. Like in *Civilization*, this carries the players forward.

In my own game, The Fog of War,[9] a simulation of the European theater of World War II, players cannot just launch attacks.

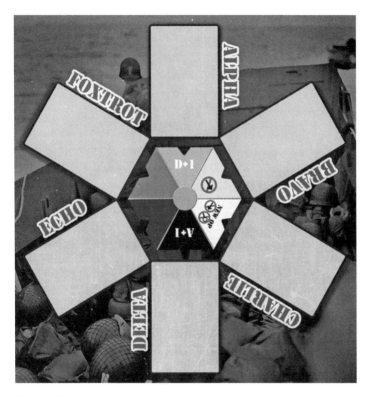

Figure 5.2
Allied operation wheel from The Fog of War.

Instead, they need to plan what are called *operations*. Forces in The Fog of War are represented by cards (see figure 5.2). Players also have a deck of cards representing the different locations they can attack. To plan an operation, they place a stack of cards that include the forces they want to attack with and the target location. But the operation cannot be launched right away. Players must wait at least two turns before they can launch the attack, and they may wait up to six turns. Each turn you wait, you may add more strength to the operation—but your opponent may conduct intelligence against it in an attempt to learn the operation's target.

Also, you are only allowed to create one new operation each turn. This evokes the same feeling as in *Civilization*, in which you have a series of partially finished projects with staggered end points.

The Fog of War also features short turns. Players have hands of three cards. On their turn, they can play any number of cards from their hand, then draw back up to three. For experienced players, a turn usually takes less than a minute. Compare that with Rise and Decline of the Third Reich,[10] in which one player's turn could easily take an hour. Turns in The Fog of War move back and forth quickly, which, as in *Civilization*, keeps the players engaged and gives the game a strong feeling of forward progress and momentum.

Through the years, designers of all types of games—video games, tabletop games, card games, and more—have realized the power of short actions that extend across turns to motivate players. Games in which players take extremely long turns while other players watch have thankfully become a small minority of new designs.

6 Regret and Competence

One of the primary motivators of human behavior is avoiding regret. Before Kahneman and Tversky formalized prospect theory and loss aversion, they believed that regret avoidance was at the root of the human behaviors they were studying.[1] They learned that there are behaviors that regret avoidance could not explain and were led to a broader picture. However, it is worth delving deeper into the dynamic of regret, which has direct applicability to game design.

Legacy Games

The box for Risk: Legacy[2] is sealed with a sticker that says, "What's done can never be undone." (See figure 6.1.)

Then, when setting up the game for the first time, one of the first things you do is choose between two special faction power stickers to place on a faction card. The rules then tell you to destroy the other one, and they are quite explicit about what *destroy* means: "If a card is DESTROYED, it is removed from the game permanently. Rip it up. Throw it in the trash."

This begins a series of one-way decisions the players need to make. They write on the board in marker, add stickers to spaces,

Figure 6.1
Risk: Legacy box sticker.

and tear up cards. In the end, they are left with a game that is unique to their group, but it is also littered with the ghosts of other choices the players could have made but did not. Forcing the players to make physical changes to the board ups the emotional stakes—and also slyly subverts our expectations about how we interact with a board game.

When people make a choice, they are frequently left with unease about the choices they leave behind, the roads not taken. In psychology, this is formally called *regret*, and it is a form of loss aversion.

Permanent choices, even simple ones like tearing up a playing card you didn't select, can make people uneasy, and they may agonize over the decision. Risk: Legacy and its progeny (collectively called *legacy games*) are designed to be played a finite number of times before the story or journey is complete (fifteen times for Risk: Legacy; from twelve to twenty-four times for Pandemic: Legacy[3]). There is a subculture of gamers who go to great lengths not to destroy cards or mark up the board, using clear overlays, numbered baggies, and other techniques to make it possible to reset the game back to its out-of-the-box configuration so that it can be played through again. Although they maintain that it is about preserving the investment they made in the game (so that it can be enjoyed again by another group), the discomfort of cutting off potential futures and the possibility of rectifying mistakes certainly plays an equally large, if not larger, role in their decision.

Except for the simplest ones, like Candy Land,[4] there is always an element of choice in games—and wherever there is choice, there is the possibility of regret. But there are many types of choices in games, from those with great strategic impact on the game, like moves in chess, to choices that are purely luck-based but may have an impact on the player personally, like deciding what number to bet on in roulette.

There is a taxonomy of choices and how they lead to different levels of potential regret. But before examining these, let's take a look at a simple game to shine a bit more light on the psychology of regret.

Regret Game

I have two dice—one red, one white—and two identical cups. I secretly place one die under each cup (no trickery), mix them up, and ask you to select the cup with the red die. You did not see me put the dice under the cups, so you have absolutely no information on which to base your decision. If you make the right choice, I give you five dollars. If not, you gain nothing.

Go ahead and select one of the cups. Let's say you pick the cup on the right. I slide it toward you but don't let you look underneath.

I then ask you if you want to switch to the cup on the left, to change your choice.

Would you switch? The majority of people do not; about 90 percent do not switch, according to studies.[5] Personally, I do this experiment with my class and at other presentations, and I have yet to have someone switch when offered the opportunity.

Why is that? The odds of being right are fifty-fifty, so why not switch?

Experimenters point to two reasons. First is the endowment effect described in chapter 2. Once you select a cup, it subtly becomes yours—and it becomes more valuable to you than the other cup. Moving the cup so that it is in front of you amplifies this effect, as the cup is moved into your personal space.

The second reason is that, psychologically, one of the drivers of our actions is our effort to minimize regret. If we make a choice and it turns out to be wrong, we feel bad. But what if we make a choice, switch, and then find out our first decision was actually correct? We feel worse. We know this about ourselves, and so, when presented with the option to switch away from our cup, it is not very enticing to do so.

We can explore exactly how much worse we feel if we switch and are wrong through a simple experiment.

In our game, if you pick the cup that has the red die, you win five dollars. Now let's say I change the rules slightly. After you've made your cup choice, I give you the option of switching to the other cup as usual. But now, if you switch and are correct, you win six dollars. If you stick with your original choice and are right, you still only get five dollars. Would you switch now?

Again, most people would not switch.

What if I offered you ten dollars if you switch and win? What about fifteen dollars?

Researchers have performed these experiments, and the results are illuminating. At triple the value, 50 percent of people switch. You need to get to ten times the value before 90 percent of people switch.

Experiments like this, by the way, are one of the methods that researchers use to figure out how much worse loss aversion makes things feel. This puts it at around three times as bad, which is in line with the two to three times values seen in other experiments.

When I was in school and taking multiple choice exams, the advice was always to "stick with your first instinct" rather than to change to a different answer. I am now convinced that this advice does not give you a better chance at getting the correct answer—but it does make people feel better than if they get it wrong and find out their original choice was correct. I would much prefer getting it wrong with my first guess than changing away from the right answer!

Regret as a Game Design Tool

As a designer, depending on the emotional stakes you want from your players, choices can be tuned to different levels. Here are the characteristics of choices that may be prone to inducing more regret:

- Being irrevocable
- Having a major impact on the game
- Offering fewer options
- Having a clear cause and effect between decision and outcome

The first two should be clear, but let's take a closer look at the last two. If the player has to choose between two options, or many options, the chances for regret vary. They are much greater with only two options. As a thought experiment, think about placing a bet on a roulette table. Let's say that on one spin you place a bet on the number 17, and it comes up 31. Then on the next spin you place a bet on red, and it comes up black.

Most likely, you would feel more regret at losing the latter bet than the former. With thirty-six possible numbers to bet on, your responsibility for making the "correct" choice is diffuse. It doesn't sting as badly when your choice goes awry. However, with a red/black bet, there are only two options—so if you lose, it's easy to picture yourself as having made the correct decision. In psychology, this is known as a *near miss*, and it is much more emotionally impactful than being far away from the correct choice. If I bet on 17, I feel much more regret if the spin comes up 16 than I do if it comes up 21. With only two options, you either win or get a near miss.

Near misses in games that you can play repeatedly have actually been shown to motivate continued play.[6] They generate a negative emotion (regret) along with a positive one (motivation). Video slot machines are specifically designed to take advantage of this effect. Because the animation of the wheels is strictly under computer control, once the random number generator decides the player has lost, the animation of the wheels stopping is designed to show the player that they almost won—just being one symbol away from winning.[7] This is such a powerful effect that some jurisdictions have started to outlaw machines that do this, but it's still legal in most places.

The last criterion on the list for having more regret is a clear linkage between the decision and the outcome. With many decisions in games, it isn't clear what the actual impact on the game is. This is particularly true as the number of decisions players make increases and the number of options for each decision increases. Both will create a disconnect between the decisions and the final result. Many games feature a series of microdecisions. These do not tend to be games that engender regret.

Let's look at a game that *does* create a strong sense of regret in the player. Lost Cities,[8] by Reiner Knizia, is a card game for two players (figure 6.2). In it, players are running expeditions to reach archeological sites represented by five different suits. Players begin an expedition by placing a card down on the table. In future turns, they may add to one of their expeditions by adding a card of the same suit but a higher number than the last card played to the expedition. At the end of the game, each expedition is worth the sum of all the cards played to it, minus twenty points.

Knizia is a mathematician by training, and many of his games, particularly the early ones, have a simple mathematical twist that makes the game. In Lost Cities, the twist is that twenty

Figure 6.2
Lost Cities.

points are deducted from each expedition. If you start a new expedition with a 1 card, you now have an expedition worth negative nineteen points. You're already in the hole. But if you don't have an expedition of a certain color, it's not worth negative twenty points; it's simply worth 0.

The crux of the game is taking calculated risks—specifically the risk that you will be able to add enough cards to an expedition to climb out of that hole and earn the points you need to win the game. Early in the game, it's likely that you will be able to get enough cards played to an expedition to score positive points. But as the game progresses through the midgame, starting a new expedition becomes more fraught.

Ultimately, this can lead to a decision the player regrets. This decision has all the hallmarks noted earlier:

- It is irrevocable. Once you start a new expedition, that card is locked down. There is no opportunity to cancel it. It is on the table and will be there for the remainder of the game.

- It has a major impact on the game. Scoring negative nineteen will almost certainly cause you to lose the game.

- There are only two options. Either you start a new expedition, or you add to an existing one.

- The connection between you starting, or not starting, an expedition and the points it scores or loses is clear. At the end of the game, it's very easy to point to the decision that led to your victory or defeat.

All these factors combine to turn what is, at its heart, a very simple card game into an emotional roller coaster as you wrestle with simple, but not simplistic, choices.

Regret and Endowed Progress

A decision that presents the opportunity for regret slows down choice. People need to think harder about it as they try to disentangle the rational from the emotional response. Some features that make decisions more prone to regret are importance and permanence. If you can't go back and change things later, it's harder to make that choice.

To keep the game moving and lighten the emotional stakes, game designers typically avoid including decisions that are prone to triggering regret. However, there are certain games in which the designer wants to bring forth these emotions, like Risk: Legacy. There, the emotional engagement of permanent decisions immediately causes players to adopt a certain mindset.

In one sense, regret is the flip side of endowed progress and the techniques we discussed in the last chapter. Endowed progress is about making positive effects more likely to happen by moving the player toward the goal. In addition, these are outcomes that, if they occur, will definitely be positive. If you get eight additional stamps, you will get the free car wash. If you get eight more victory points, you will win the game. If you get to three thousand experience points, you will go up a level.

Choices that lead to regret are negative, even if the effects are positive. In Risk: Legacy, the players need to choose between one of two special abilities. Both are positive, and both make that faction more powerful. But the other needs to be ripped up and destroyed, and it's impossible for the players to know what the future would have held if they had chosen that other ability. The loss, in this case, is not for something tangible but for a potential future—which mirrors some of the most difficult choices we make in life.

Endowed progress is the opposite of this. Other options are not eliminated; endowed progress is about moving toward a singular goal. Regret typically comes from big choices made at a crossroads, whereas endowed progress breaks things up into small chunks that are easy to deal with. It is not surprising that one creates angst while the other motivates.

Massively multiplayer online (MMO) games, like *World of Warcraft*,[9] create regret in their structure. They often force players to make certain decisions about skills and other options when new levels are reached, and these are decisions that have far-reaching and long-term implications for characters that may be played for years. This leads to players stressing over how to advance their characters, agonizing over the distribution of each point. Two mechanisms have arisen in an attempt to alleviate the regret that these choices can generate: one from the community and one from within the games themselves.

Because this is the age of the internet, there is a plethora of resources available to players on how to design their characters (called *builds* or *specs*). These range from calculators that show how your character will perform when certain skills and spells are chosen to complete recipes for what the "best" character design is to fulfill certain roles or play styles. Selecting one of these gives partial immunity to regret. It gives players a glimpse into the future, more visibility into what they can expect. Psychologically, it allows for shifting blame to the author of the build guide if the player doesn't get the satisfaction or performance they were expecting. This ignores the fact that in-game performance relies on more than just the skills chosen; it also relies on the skill of the player. But again, it gives psychological cover to the player and one less thing for them to worry about, which reduces prospective regret. These types of guides go well beyond MMOs. They also are very influential in the world of Magic: The Gathering deck creation (*net decking*) and miniatures games, in which army composition lists on popular sites are very influential.

The other element that helps ease regret is the ability in some games to perform a *respec*, via which a character can be completely rebuilt from the ground up. These are usually earned at certain points in character development or can be purchased or are sometimes given when character abilities are modified in their ability or power. Regardless of the source, this is a powerful antidote to regret. Making decisions about your character development with the knowledge that they are not irrevocable does wonders to quell regret, even if the potential for such a respec is well in the future.

The rise of battle royale games like *Fortnite* and *PlayerUnknown's Battlegrounds* (*PUBG*)[10] present an interesting case study on regret, and loss aversion more generally.[11] These games feature permadeath, which should increase player anxiety and works against these being for casual players. However, there are several factors that mitigate the psychology—but first, let's take a brief look at the format: Battle royale games have up to one hundred players in the same game, playing either individually or as small squads of two or three people. When a player is killed, they are eliminated from the game, and may not return. When only one player (or squad) remains, they win the game. To force player interaction, the play area shrinks over the course of the game, driving players together into the same area.

Now, the first mitigating feature of a battle royale is its length. The games typically take fifteen to twenty minutes in to complete, thanks to the ever-shrinking field. Many players are eliminated much earlier, giving them a minimal time investment. There's a big difference between permadeath after five minutes and after five hours.

The second, and perhaps more significant, factor is the structure of the game itself. The longer that players last in the game, the better they are doing. The number of players remaining is prominently displayed in the corner of the screen in all these games, and merely surviving as that number ticks down is gratifying. Length both increases the stakes, as you get closer to possibly winning, and decreases them, as you have already done better than so many others in the game. And given that one hundred players are in each game, casual players go in with realistic expectations about their chances of winning.

Competence

In addition to thinking about possible future regret, decisions are also impacted by how much information people feel they have available to make the decision. This is called *Competence*. Before getting into the details of exactly what that means, let's look at a simple game. Two games, actually; you can decide which one you want to play. The objective in both games is the same: guess if a die roll is even or odd. Here are the choices:

Game 1

You guess whether the roll of a die will be even or odd. Then I roll a die, and we see if you're right.

Game 2

I secretly roll a die and put it under a cup. Then you guess if the roll will be even or odd, I lift the cup, and you see if you're right.

When presented with this choice, most people—almost 67 percent—select game 1. This seems peculiar at first. Why should there be a preference for one over the other? The chances of winning the game are 50 percent either way. What is the difference?

This illustrates a concept that is referred to as "competence". *Competence* is defined (semimathematically) as the amount of information you have before making a decision divided by the total amount of information that can possibly be known. In the game 1, you know everything there is to know about the situation. But in the second, there is a key fact that exists in the universe—what the die result is—that you don't know. So, your competence in game 2 is much lower than it is in game 1.

Studies have shown that people much prefer high competence situations, even when competence has no bearing on the outcome. Low competence makes people uneasy and ties into the same psychological circuits that make us avoid regret and loss.

Here's another game choice:

Game 1

I give you a box with fifty red balls and fifty green balls. You name a color and then blindly pull out a ball. If it matches your chosen color, you win.

Game 2

I give you a box. It is guaranteed to have at least one ball but could hold any number. And all the balls in the box are either red or green, but I'm not telling you the distribution. They could all be red, or all green, or a fifty-fifty mix, or anything in between. The game is the same as game 1: you name a color, blindly pull out a ball, and if it matches your chosen color, you win.

Which game would you rather play?

The chances of winning either game are 50 percent. This is obvious for game 1 but might need some explanation for game 2. How can it be 50 percent with so many unknown variables? The key is that the player gets a choice of which color they are trying to pull from the box. Because the contents of the box can't be changed after this choice is made, there's no way to set up the balls in such a way that overall there isn't a 50 percent chance of winning.

As an example, let's say I put five red balls in the box—that's it. Assuming that you, as the player, have an equal chance of announcing that your target is red or green, then 50 percent of the time you pick red, giving you a 100 percent chance to win—and 50 percent of the time you pick green, with a 0 percent chance to win. So your overall win rate is $(0.5)*(1) + (0.5)*(0) = 0.5$. The general equation for a box that has X fraction of red balls and $(1-X)$ fraction of green balls is $(0.5)*(X) + (0.5)*(1-X)$, which is always 0.5 regardless of X.

Even when this is explained to people, over 90 percent pick game 1. The uncertainty makes the second game much less attractive. People are more likely to think that there is some trick they aren't understanding, that they are being duped. Game 1 is clear: fifty balls of each type, and you have a gut feeling for what your options are.

But even in less extreme cases, research has shown that people gravitate toward the option in which there is the least amount of hidden information, as illustrated in the first "die under a cup" example.

Attack/Defend Example: Who Chooses First?

Let's take this principle and apply it to a simple fighting game.

There are two players: an attacker and a defender. The attacker has two choices: punch and kick. The defender also has two choices: block high and block low. Block high counters a punch and block low counters a kick. You have cards representing the choices, and you have to pick one and place it face down in front of you.

Would you prefer to play first or second in this situation? From an outcome standpoint, it doesn't make a difference— unless you have some sort of tell that helps your opponent figure you out. But when surveyed, 65 percent of people preferred to go first. This preference is what we would expect based on competence theory. If you go first, you know all the information there is to know in the world. But if you play second, there's a big piece of knowledge that you don't have access to—what your opponent has chosen. This makes it a much more emotionally fraught decision for many people.

From a design perspective, this allows the designer to manipulate the emotional state of the players and make decisions harder or easier.

Video Games versus Board Games

A key characteristic of the majority of board games is that the game space is completely known. Maybe you don't know the order in which the cards will come up, but the range of possible cards is knowledge that players have—certainly after they've played the game a few times, but also you can simply pick up the deck between games and look at all the cards. Maybe you don't know what you'll roll on the dice, but you know what the possible outcomes of that roll are. In general, board gamers are used to high competence situations.

In the 1970s and 1980s, war games from companies like Avalon Hill and Simulations Publications, Inc. (SPI) were becoming more complex because complexity was equated (often erroneously) with realism in military simulations. However, these games reached a level at which it was difficult for players to manage systems that required increasing amounts of bookkeeping.

When computers became increasingly available in the 1990s, war gamers were excited about the prospect of games being moved to that platform. The computer would handle all the tedious bookkeeping, allowing players to focus on the strategies and tactics. As computers became more powerful, computer war games tracked more and more stats. *Carrier Strike*[12] tracked the fuel in each aircraft in the air, the fatigue level of individual pilots, and how many planes were on each deck of the carrier. *The Operational Art of War*[13] kept track of the exact mix of weaponry in entire battalions—as well as detailed tracking of supplies, fatigue, and disorganization (see figure 6.3). And all this information was available to players. All the data could be accessed and reviewed by the players when making decisions about what to do in the game.

However, the level of detail exceeded the capacity of most players to deal with it effectively. It ended up being a fog of data, and players retreated from it, abstracting it in their minds. It flipped around and became a negative: players were aware that this data existed but were not able to take advantage of it in any meaningful way. Ironically, even though all the data *could be known*, this triggered a feeling of low competence and all the negative emotions and uncertainty that come along with that.

Figure 6.3

Unit report from *The Operational Art of War*. The unit itself is composed of various assets, each of which has its own statistics (lower left).

This type of war game became a dead end, development-wise. There were further attempts to incorporate this level of detail, but they attracted a limited audience. There is a limit to how much information people can absorb and act upon, and giving players more information leads to blow back and reduced enjoyment. The design space shifted toward more abstraction—or at least smarter abstractions that represented realism by focusing on the information and decisions that would be available to actual commanders at the level being simulated. The *Combat Mission*[14] series of games has the players issuing orders to troops and tanks—and then sitting back to watch a movie of the action unfolding. The game gives high-level information about the status of various units but, ultimately, does not give the player access to detailed information about each soldier or how many inches of armor plating was penetrated. Instead, simple status indicators show "disorder" levels (like Good Order or Panic), and the player works with that information.

An interesting feature of these systems is that they don't reveal to the player exactly what these status indicators mean, for example, to the firepower of the unit. The percentage reduction of strength for different statuses is built into the software, but it isn't revealed to the players—as it would have to be in a board game in which the players are responsible for resolving combat.

However, this doesn't feel as much like a loss of competence because in the real world we are used to this type of uncertainty when dealing with people. So we fall back on predispositions and then gradually adjust our mental model within the context of the game as we gain more experience with how those units behave. Being able to map into real-world experience keeps away feelings of low competence.

Many video games take advantage of the players' feelings of low competence by giving players the chance to repeat encounters and gradually learn the patterns behind what is happening on screen, which ultimately enables them to succeed. This typically happens with boss fights, the biggest challenges of many games.

Dark Souls[15] is a classic example of this genre. When players face a new boss, they enter the encounter with extremely low competence. The boss has special attacks, and as it takes damage from the players it will change its patterns and modes of attacking until defeated. When first encountering a boss, players have no idea what to do. They need to be close observers and experiment with different techniques to determine the weaknesses of each particular one.

Normally, one would expect that these encounters, which start with low competence, would result in negative player reactions. However, designers adopt several techniques to avoid this and instead leverage low competence to increase the sense of accomplishment of the players.

First, there is predictability and repetition in the boss's actions. It performs certain attacks and moves to new attacks in a definite progression, so its patterns can be learned. The learning happens on both a macro level—learning the types of attack patterns the boss moves through as it becomes damaged—and on a micro level by predicting specific attacks.

This leads to the second technique: telegraphing. Through actions, graphical cues, or sound cues, the players begin to learn how to predict which attacks come next. There is also feedback indicating damage levels and when a boss will shift to its next set of attack patterns.

Both techniques let players know that they have low competence at the start of the fight—but that with skill and observation, they can increase that competence until it reaches a level where they win the encounter. Having this type of learning and advancement has been shown to be a primary motivator for player engagement in games.

So as a designer, it is important to be aware that low competence itself is not a negative. The problem is low competence that stays low. If the players have a natural path to increase competence as the game goes on, that dynamic can flip from demotivating to highly motivational. However, if handled incorrectly, low competence can indeed be a negative. The game *Cuphead*[16] is a highly rated game in the "run and gun" genre, in which players need to master precise movements and learn to anticipate boss patterns to succeed. Its inventive characters and vintage art style have attracted many players who are not used to a game this punishing, and these players end up frustrated. But even among run and gun aficionados, *Cuphead* has garnered criticism about two specific design choices leading to low competence in the players.[17]

First, the levels have random elements that can put players into no-win situations. The game demands precision from players and rewards careful play, but, on some levels, the game builds in randomness that works against player precision by having the chance of random enemy movements that make death inevitable. This takes knowledge of what is to come away from the player and puts it behind a random number generator. Randomness does not foster low competence in and of itself; think back to our first die-rolling example. But random sequences that may create no-win situations emphasize uncertainty about the "facts in the world" (in this case, not the randomness itself, but the way different random elements may interact in the future), giving the player feelings of doubt and discomfort.

The second element is more direct. The bosses in *Cuphead* do not have a health bar, and most do not have a graphical indication of how close they are to being defeated. If the player loses, the game does show them how close they were to defeating the boss—so players can begin to get a sense of a boss's health. But in the heat of the battle, this is not shown. This takes away an important tool from the players, and the boss's health is a definite fact about the world they don't know. Plus, if it were known, it would (positively) impact players. If you know that one or two more hits will win the battle, you can change your playstyle to take more chances.

Regret and low competence are comparable in the way that they can make it difficult for people to make decisions, but they are typically on opposite ends of the decision spectrum. Regret is caused by having just a few choices with clear possible outcomes. Low competence is caused when the inputs and outputs of the decision are fuzzy and unknown. Regret can be a useful tool in game design, but, in general, sustained low competence (not low competence that can be overcome through learning) should be avoided. It leads to a general feeling of helplessness and will strongly demotivate players.

7   Putting It All Together

In the introduction, I posed this question:

> **How does the designer create the desired player experience? How can the emotions of the players be steered onto the desired path?**

Loss aversion is a surprisingly versatile tool to achieve a wide variety of experiences. The core of loss aversion is simple: losing feels worse than gaining feels good. But designers can spin this simple core into a vast array of player emotions by working with or against people's natural inclinations:

- People prefer sure gains over a chance for a larger gain.
- People will take a risk to avoid a sure loss.
- People treat all small probabilities the same and just compare the gain or loss.
- Both 100 percent and 0 percent are special.
- Things that people own gain more value in their eyes. Personalizing or anthropomorphizing enhances this effect.
- People give less value to tokens and other abstract representations of value than to actual money they are familiar with.
- Choices can be manipulated to feel good or bad to people by framing them as gains or losses.

- When values get very large or very small, people mentally lump them together.
- If people first win, then lose, they will make different choices than if they first lose, then win.
- Giving people a little bit of progress toward a goal will make them much more motivated to complete tasks to achieve that goal.
- Making a decision when there is hidden information makes people uncomfortable.
- People do not like to make choices that are big, irrevocable, and have a clear impact.

There's an important caveat for everything discussed in this book: these studies describe tendencies, not absolute truth for all people. Think back to the first formal study question posed:

> Which would you rather have?
>
> (A) An 80 percent chance of winning $4,000.
> (B) A 100 percent chance of winning $3,000.

If 80 percent of people answered B, that means that 20 percent of people answered A—or one in five. So there is an excellent chance that in almost any multiplayer game, there will be people who don't respond the way the designer expects them to—or don't get the intended emotional impact.

And most of the studies had results in the 65 percent range, meaning that one out of three people responded the other way. The car wash study resulted in 34 percent of people redeeming one coupon, compared to 17 percent who redeemed the other. But 66 percent of people still never bothered to get the free wash. My twelve-year-old niece recently played *Portal* and tossed the Weighted Companion Cube into the fire without a second thought.

Everything that's discussed in this book is a tendency and doesn't affect everyone the same way. The reaction depends on the environment, the type of day the player had, and so many other factors. Incorporating the emotional triggers related to loss aversion may nudge players in certain directions, but, as they say, your results may vary.

The ultimate goal of understanding loss aversion and its associated techniques is not to ensure only positive emotions or only negative ones. No emotion is always right or wrong to incorporate into a design. And though properly tuning the emotional palette of the game will not guarantee that it succeeds or is popular, having an emotional mismatch will certainly result in the opposite.

There are many elements that go into game design, and all of them are critical to the user experience. User interface, story, artwork, sound, game mechanics, difficulty curve, feedback loops—each is incredibly important in its own way. Loss aversion is a piece of this puzzle—and often a hidden piece. Testers may be able to point to why controls were difficult to use or why a particular puzzle was too obscure, but they may not realize why a certain decision rubbed them the wrong way or made them anxious. Designers should be familiar with the reasons behind these amorphous concerns and, even better, to design things in the first place that utilize these techniques effectively from the start.

The Agricola Series

The game Agricola,[1] designed by Uwe Rosenberg, has been a top-rated game since its release. Themed around medieval subsistence farming, it challenges the players to use their limited workers (initially two, more if you have children) to expand the family farm and avoid starvation. Rosenberg has released two games building on the theme and mechanics of Agricola: Caverna[2] in 2013 and A Feast for Odin[3] in 2016. Looking at what was changed in these subsequent games—and the impact these changes have on the player experience—illustrates many of the themes of this book.[4]

At the end of Agricola, you score points from various aspects of your farm. You get points for having animals, pastures, vegetables, and more. The score summary from the game outlines this, as shown in figure 7.1. Notice, however, that you're penalized if you're missing any of the elements. No sheep means you lose a point, and you also lose points by having undeveloped areas in your farmyard.

Scoring	-1 Point	1 Point	2 Points	3 Points	4 Points
Fields	0-1	2	3	4	5+
Pastures	0	1	2	3	4+
Grain*	0	1-3	4-5	6-7	8+
Vegetables*	0	1	2	3	4+
Sheep	0	1-3	4-5	6-7	8+
Wild boar	0	1-2	3-4	5-6	7+
Cattle	0	1	2-3	4-5	6+

*Planted & harvested Grain / Vegetables

-1 point per unused space in the Farmyard
1 point per fenced stable & per Clay hut room
2 points per Stone house room
3 points per Family member

Figure 7.1
Agricola score card.

The design goal of this somewhat convoluted system is to push players to diversify their farms, which presents an interesting challenge because specialization makes players the most efficient. So there's a balance there. But as you can expect, these penalties create a negative emotion in players: first-timers often forget about them, and experienced players worry and work hard to avoid them whenever possible. These are clearly framed as losses.

In Caverna, this dynamic is softened a bit. Penalties are only given for missing farm animals and for empty spaces, not for the other elements of the farm. Rosenberg removed over half of the loss aversion elements in scoring.

For Odin, Rosenberg took a different tack. Rather than having players lose points for not being diverse, he represents penalties geometrically on a player board. Instead of growing vegetables and getting farm animals, players have to acquire goods, represented by different colored polyomino pieces of varying sizes. These are then

Figure 7.2
A Feast for Odin player board. The −1 spaces can be seen in the grid on the left.

placed on the player board, starting from one corner and building outward (see figure 7.2). Spread across the board are spaces with a –1 symbol. At the end of the game, the player loses points for the –1 spaces that are not covered by goods tiles. In addition, goods tiles of certain colors may not be placed next to one another.

This accomplishes two things. First, by requiring that different color tiles abut, it enforces diversity in what goods players acquire. Next, by putting the negative spaces in front of players right from the start and having those spaces be covered as the game goes on, an end game negative is turned into an in-game positive.

This is a terrific example of framing. By putting the negatives right out in the open, players can only gain points as the game goes on. They are at their worst right at the start, and then they build up from there. It also gives great positive feedback as the game progresses because players are able to purchase bigger tiles and cover a larger number of negative spaces at the same time. This process gives an emotional lift to the players, who can shed losses more easily as the game progresses.

Rosenberg could have taken this one step further and switched the negative spaces to positive spaces, so the players would gain bonus points as the spaces became covered instead of losing negative points. Mathematically it would be the same: players who did not hit a bonus space would still be a point behind their opponents who did. It is possible that Rosenberg kept negative points in Odin to preserve the lineage of negative points from Agricola and Caverna. Perhaps it would have been simply a step too far in the evolution. However, it is also possible that he believed the negative points created a stronger drive to cover them up. Loss aversion tells us that eliminating negative points is more motivating than gaining bonus points and that players will work harder to achieve that goal. So maintaining this feature drives player behavior to remain focused on that aspect of the game, which the designer may have decided was part of his vision for the player experience.

A second aspect that evolved was feeding your people. In Agricola, you must have two food units for each of your workers at increasingly frequent intervals. For each food you are short, you need to take a Begging card, which causes you to lose three points at the end of the game. Your workers don't actually starve and get eliminated from the game; it's simply a point penalty assessed at the end.

But the feeding phase does trigger emotion in the way it's framed. Your workers are family (they are called *family members*). The action that creates a new worker is called the *family action*, and your new worker can't work at first but only needs half the food, an obvious analogy to having a child. Despite the workers being flat wooden discs, the game takes pains to personify them as a family on a family farm.

Not having enough food to feed them at the end of a season feels very personal. And sometimes you will need to sacrifice things to avoid starvation, which may still generate feelings of loss. For example, you may have to eat the vegetables you were hoping to plant next season for more crops—or slaughter an animal for the meat, which may prevent your animals from breeding. These are very visceral choices that definitely trigger loss aversion in the players. On the positive side, the need to feed your family does give new players a clear, early goal in a dizzying array of options. You need to have a certain amount of food in a certain number of turns. You have focus immediately, which helps get players acclimated to the game.

In Caverna, the system is similar to Agricola. However, there are more ways to generate food, so it is a bit simpler to get everyone fed—allowing players to focus on the many additional activities added by Caverna, such as mining and exploration.

Odin preserves the need to feed your workers but twists it around, again via framing. First, the feeding phase is now called the *feast phase*. You are not failing to provide food to your family but simply failing to adequately provide for a feast. And you no longer gain Begging cards. They are now called *Thing Penalties*,[5] which is much more neutral. *Begging* is very much a loaded term with negative connotations.

In addition, the mechanism for feeding is based on placing tiles on a *banquet table*, similar to the way goods tiles are placed on the main player board. And these also come in various widths, making it more viscerally satisfying (and intuitively obvious) to see how close you are to fulfilling the feast requirement.

Finally, silver coins, which are a wildcard resource, can be used as a way of making it easier to fulfill the feasting requirement in Odin.

These changes, taken together, make it much less likely that players will fail at feeding their workers. The rules specifically say, "This should not happen too often, because the feast happens after you receive income. Income should always provide enough silver to cover the spaces." There is no similar assurance in either Agricola or Caverna.

The final element illustrating Rosenberg's progression are the workers themselves. Called family members in Agricola, dwarves in Caverna, and Vikings in A Feast for Odin, using these is the core way that players do things in the game. For example, placing a worker on an action space allows a player to immediately take that action. In Agricola, placing a worker on a Gain 3 Stone space allows you to take three stone tokens.

At the start of Agricola, you have two workers. This creates a situation that is primed for regret. The main drivers for regret are decisions that are irrevocable, limited, important, and clear. Here we have all those ingredients. You only have two opportunities to pick something from a limited menu. The action is done immediately and cannot be undone. There are some spaces that give a choice of actions, but the player must immediately decide what to do. And with the threat of starvation, the importance of the decisions—and how they impact your ability to get enough food—is clear. This tendency for regret is strong and does not lessen as the game progresses—despite players building up engines to create food, like flocks of animals, and adding more family members—because the number of turns between harvests (when players need to eat) decreases throughout the game.

The system in Caverna is similar, although because food is less of an issue, the individual decisions feel less consequential. But you still start with only two workers.

In Odin, you start with five workers and automatically gain one each turn to a maximum of twelve. Counteracting this a bit, actions cost between one and four workers to perform. In Agricola and Caverna, they always cost one. This dramatically reduces the potential for regret. Having the ability to place five separate workers means that each individual decision is less important on its own. It gives the opportunity to recover from a mistake.

Having more workers also enhances the feeling of endowed progress. Agricola and Caverna, with only two workers to use each turn, make it more difficult to chain things together from micro- into macroplans. With five workers, Odin has the luxury of smaller actions that give the players more of a sense of forward momentum: they have a heightened feeling of having started on a plan that needs to be completed.

Including spaces that require varying numbers of workers also serves to signal to beginning players the relative strengths of certain actions, as well as reduce the rush for the best spaces that is seen in Agricola. These improvements are not directly related to loss aversion but are worth noting.

Taken altogether—creating negative spaces on the player board instead of negative end game scores, replacing begging with feasting, and increasing the number of workers—Uwe Rosenberg has clearly moved in the direction of reducing loss aversion and regret and enhancing endowed progress by reframing or directly modifying underlying mechanics. Although personal preferences will vary, he has decided that softening these edges creates a better experience for the players.

Conclusion

More and more, game designers aspire to sophisticated experiences and advanced narrative techniques that will take the players on a journey. My hope is that by understanding loss aversion, which is so fundamental to the human psyche, designers will be able to more directly tune the game to achieve their goals and create ever more memorable and dynamic experiences.

Notes

Introduction

1. James Ohlen, designer, *Knights of the Old Republic* (LucasArts, 2003).

2. Will Wright, designer, *SimCity* (Maxis, 1989).

3. Friedemann Friese, designer, Power Grid (2F-Spiele, 2004).

4. Joakim Bergqwist, designer, *Crusader Kings* (Paradox Entertainment, 2004).

5. Richard Garfield, designer, Magic: The Gathering (Wizards of the Coast, 1994).

6. David Brevik et al., designers, *Diablo* (Blizzard Entertainment, 1996).

7. Preston Watamaniuk, designer, *Mass Effect* (Bioware, 2007).

8. David Chircop and Yannick Massa, designers, *… and then, we held hands* (LudiCreations, 2015).

9. Greg Costikyan, *Uncertainty in Games* (Cambridge, MA: MIT Press, 2013).

1   Loss Aversion

1. Daniel Kahneman and Amos Tversky, "Prospect Theory: An Analysis of Decision under Ris," *Econometrica* 47, no. 2 (March 1979): 263–291.

2. *Expectation value* is the average gain if the choice is made over and over again. Sometimes you gain $4,000; sometimes you gain nothing; but on average you will gain $3,200.

3. See Lotteryusa.com.

4. Toru Iwatani, creator, *Pac-Man* (Namco, 1980).

5. Uncredited designer, *Ms. Pac-Man* (Midway, 1982).

6. Christine Love, creator, *Hate Plus* (Love Conquers All Games, 2013).

7. Andrew Greenberg and Robert Woodhead, creators, *Wizardry* (Sir-Tech, 1982).

8. Richard Garriott, creator, *Ultima* (Origin Systems, 1981).

9. Tyler Sigman, designer, *Darkest Dungeon* (Red Hook Studios, 2016).

10. Gary Gygax and Dave Arneson, creators, Dungeons & Dragons (TSR, 1974).

11. See tvtropes.org/pmwiki/pmwiki.php/Main/LevelDrain.

12. Daniel Kahneman, Jack L. Knetsch, and Richard H. Thaler, "Anomalies: The Endowment Effect, Loss Aversion, and Status Quo Bias," *Journal of Economic Perspectives* 5, no. 1 (Winter 1991): 193–206.

13. Christina Norman et al., designers, *League of Legends* (Riot Games, 2009).

14. Uncredited designer, *Eve Online* (CCP Games, 2003).

15. Dustin Browder and Alan Dabiri, directors, *Heroes of the Storm* (Blizzard Entertainment, 2015).

16. These include the 0 in roulette or the push on a 12 in craps.

2 Endowment Effect

1. Jack Knetsch and J. A. Sinden, "Willingness to Pay and Compensation Demanded: Experimental Evidence of an Unexpected Disparity

on Measures of Value," *Quarterly Journal of Economics* 99, no. 3 (August 1984): 507–521.

2. Richard Thaler, "Toward a Positive Theory of Consumer Choice," *Journal of Economic Behavior & Organization* 1, no. 1 (March 1980): 39–60. In 2017, Thaler was awarded the Nobel Prize in Economics for this work.

3. Mugs are particularly popular in endowment effect experiments, for reasons that are a mystery to the author.

4. Sarah Brosnan et al., "Endowment Effects in Chimpanzees," *Current Biology* 17, no. 19 (October 2007): 1704–1707.

5. Brian Knutson et al., "Neural Antecedents of the Endowment Effect," *Neuron* 58, no. 5 (June 2008): 814–822.

6. Kim Swift, designer, *Portal* (Valve, 2007).

7. Joshua Weier, project lead, *Portal 2* (Valve, 2011).

8. See https://web.archive.org/web/20160202110657/http://1up.com/features/beyond-the-box.

9. See http://metagearsolid.org/reports_fromnothing2.html.

10. Ignacy Trzewiczek, creator, *Robinson Crusoe* (Portal Games, 2012).

11. Ignacy Trzewiczek, designer, *First Martians* (Portal Games, 2017).

12. See https://www.boardgamegeek.com/thread/995656/yep-youre-doomed-sessionreview-robinson-crusoe-adv.

13. See https://www.boardgamegeek.com/thread/1843786/core-issues-first-martians-math-cruel-and-thematic.

14. Michael Toy et al., creators, *Rogue* (freeware, 1980).

15. Julian Gollop and Nick Gollop, designers, *X-COM: UFO Defense* (Mythos, 1994).

16. Shouzou Kaga, designer, *Fire Emblem: Shadow Dragon and the Blade of Light* (Nintendo, 1990).

17. See http://kotaku.com/fire-emblem-players-permadeath-or-no-per madeath-1760822661.

18. Yoshinori Kitase, director, *Final Fantasy VII* (Square, 1997).

19. See http://kotaku.com/the-steam-achievement-that-nobody-unlocked -1610073943.

3 Framing

1. Mathematical aside:

For Choice C: 0.25 * 0.8 = 20 percent chance to win.

For Choice D: 0.25 * 1.0 = 25 percent chance to win.

2. Geoffrey Engelstein, creator, Pit Crew (Stronghold Games, 2017).

3. Geoffrey Engelstein, creator, The Expanse (WizKids Games, 2017).

4. Paul Haskell Jr. and William Storey, creators, Sorry! (Hasbro, 1929).

5. Albert Lamorisse and Michael Levin, designers, Risk (Parker Brothers, 1959).

6. Elizabeth Magie and Charles Darrow, creators, Monopoly (Parker Brothers, 1933).

7. On a personal note, my sister and I have not played Risk since the infamous Congo incident of 1980.

8. Klaus Teuber, designer, The Settlers of Catan (Kosmos, 1995).

9. See https://www.youtube.com/watch?v=YJtzAcBStLc.

10. There is a way to reduce the length of a road, interrupting it by constructing a settlement or city in the middle, but this is rare and doesn't impact the larger point.

11. Charlie Catino and Steven Kimball, designers, Nexus Ops (Avalon Hill, 2005).

12. Jacques Bariot and Guillaume Montiage, designers, Kemet (Matagot, 2012).

13. Touko Tahkokallio, designer, Eclipse (Lautapelit.fi, 2011).

14. Grant Rodiek et al., designers, Cry Havoc (Portal, 2016).

15. IceFrog, developer, *Dota 2* (Valve, 2013).

16. See http://www.gamespot.com/forums/pc-mac-linux-society-1000004/ dota-2-vs-lol-educated-comparison-29187896/ and http://gazettereview .com/2016/01/league-of-legends-vs-dota/.

17. Chris Metzen and James Phinney, designers, *Starcraft* (Blizzard, 1998).

18. Uncredited designer, *Counter-Strike: Global Offensive* (Valve, 2012).

19. Jeremy Craig et al., designers, *Overwatch* (Blizzard, 2016).

20. For more on battle royales, see chapter 6.

21. See http://fortune.com/2016/04/06/most-popular-esports-games-on -twitch/.

22. Uncredited designer, *Fortnite* (Epic Games, 2017).

4   Utility Theory

1. NBC, 2005.

2. W. W. Swilling, designer, Cosmic Wimpout (C3, 1975).

3. Traditional game, dating back to the 1930s.

4. Bruno Faidutti and Alan Moon, designers, Incan Gold (Schmidt-Spiele, 2005).

5. Sid Sackson, designer, Can't Stop (Parker Brothers, 1980).

5   Endowed Progress

1. Joseph Nunes and Xavier Dreze, "The Endowed Progress Effect: How Artificial Advancement Increases Effort," *Journal of Consumer Research* 32 (March 2006): 504–512.

2. In addition to improving the emotional state of players, the rating floor also helps prevent *sandbagging*, in which players intentionally lose to reduce their ratings so that they can enter tournaments with cash prizes intended for less-skilled players.

3. Nunes and Dreze, "The Endowed Progress Effect."

4. In the first car wash experiment, they told people that the car wash was running a special promotion that day—and that was the reason they were getting two stamps.

5. Sid Meier, creator, *Civilization* (Microprose, 1991).

6. Jim Dunnigan, designer, PanzerBlitz (Avalon Hill, 1970).

7. Chad Jensen, designer, Combat Commander: Europe (GMT, 2006).

8. Gutier Lusquiños Rodríguez, designer, Infinity (Corvus Belli, 2005).

9. Geoffrey Engelstein, designer, The Fog of War (Stronghold Games, 2016).

10. Don Greenwood and John Prados, creators, Rise and Decline of the Third Reich (Avalon Hill, 1974).

6   Regret and Competence

1. Michael Lewis, *The Undoing Project: A Friendship that Changed Our Minds* (New York: W. W. Norton, 2016).

2. Rob Daviau, designer, Risk: Legacy (Hasbro, 2011).

3. Matt Leacock and Rob Daviau, designers, Pandemic: Legacy (Z-Man Games, 2015).

4. Eleanor Abbott, designer, Candy Land (Milton Bradley, 1949).

5. Donald Granberg and Thad Brown, "The Monty Hall Dilemma," *Personality and Social Psychology Bulletin* 21, no. 7 (July 1995): 711–723.

6. R. L. Reid, "The Psychology of the Near Miss," *Journal of Gambling Behavior* 2, no. 1 (Spring/Summer 1986): 32–39.

7. Natasha Shüll, *Addiction by Design: Machine Gambling in Las Vegas* (Princeton, NJ: Princeton University Press, 2014).

8. Reiner Knizia, designer, Lost Cities (Kosmos, 1999).

9. Rob Pardo et al., designers, *World of Warcraft* (Blizzard, 2004).

10. Brendan Greene, creator, *PlayerUnknown's Battlegrounds* (PUBG, 2017).

11. I am indebted to Matt Villers, who first suggested these ideas on Twitter. See https://twitter.com/matthew_villers/status/1039313575125217280.

12. Gary Grisby, designer, *Carrier Strike: South Pacific 1942–44* (Strategic Simulations, 1992).

13. Norm Kroger, designer, *The Operational Art of War* (Talonsoft, 1998).

14. Charles Moylan and Stephen Grammont, designers, *Combat Mission: Beyond Overlord* (Battlefront, 2000).

15. Hidetaka Miyazaki, creator, *Dark Souls* (Namco Bandai, 2011).

16. Jared Moldenhauer, designer, *Cuphead* (Studio MDHR, 2017).

17. Snoman Gaming, for example; see https://www.youtube.com/watch?v=G_b3K21ulSQ.

7   Putting It All Together

1. Uwe Rosenberg, designer, Agricola (Lookout Games, 2007).

2. Uwe Rosenberg, designer, Caverna (Lookout Games, 2013).

3. Uwe Rosenberg, designer, A Feast for Odin (Lookout Games, 2016).

4. I am indebted to Grant Rodiek for much of this analysis. See http://hyperbolegames.com/blog/farm-odins-table.

5. A *Thing* was a Viking assembly.

Index

Page numbers in italics indicate references to figures.